PRAISE FOR
LESSONS FROM THE HEART
OF AMERICAN BUSINESS

"There is no substitute for experience . . . and few business executives have had a wider range of geographic and industrial business experiences than Gerald Greenwald. . . . A sophisticated observer. The 'war stories' are well told."
—Lester Thurow, economist, MIT, and author of *Building Wealth: The New Rules for Individuals, Companies, and Nations in a Knowledge-Based Economy*

"Above all, a leader must have the utmost ability to learn. Jerry Greenwald is a consummate learner, and we are fortunate to have him share his incredible awareness of his own experiences with us."
—Phil Condit, chairman and CEO, The Boeing Company

"No one has done more in using new management skills to bring together organized labor and management than Gerald Greenwald. [This book] is very instructive for those managers faced with these issues as we turn into the wind of a new century."
—Jim Barksdale, partner, The Barksdale Group

"The rarest of business biographies, infused with not only uncommon wit and wisdom but genuine warmth and humanity."
—Jason McManus, former editor-in-chief, Time Inc.

LESSONS FROM

✱

THE HEART

✱

OF AMERICAN

✱

BUSINESS

A Roadmap for Managers in the 21st Century

GERALD GREENWALD

WITH CHARLES MADIGAN

Published by Warner Books

An AOL Time Warner Company

Warner Business Books are published by Warner Books, Inc.
1271 Avenue of the Americas, New York, NY 10020

Visit our Web site at www.twbookmark.com.

 An AOL Time Warner Company

Printed in the United States of America
Originally published in hardcover by Warner Books, Inc.
First Trade Printing: April 2002
10 9 8 7 6 5 4 3 2 1

The Library of Congress has cataloged the hardcover edition as follows:
Greenwald, Gerald.
    Lessons from the heart of American business : a roadmap for managers in the 21st century / Gerald Greenwald; with Charles Madigan.
        p. cm.
    Includes index.
    ISBN 0-446-52544-8
    1. Management—United States. I. Madigan, Charles. II. Title.

HD70.U5 G694 2001
658—dc21   00-046221

ISBN 0-446-67848-1 (pbk.)

Book design by Giorgetta Bell McRee
Cover design by Flag

To my wife, Glenda, and my children—Scott, Stacey, Bradley, and Josh—who were all on this journey with me, and to my father, Frank Greenwald, who taught me life's most important lessons.

ACKNOWLEDGMENTS

───────────────✶───────────────

Whenever I finished with an interesting, exciting, or educational experience in my life, I would often say, "This will go into the book I'll never write."

I changed my mind.

I knew why I wanted to write this book. It was for my grandchildren. The tough question was, why would anyone but those close to me want to read it? As I thought about it and made notes on where I've been and what I've been fortunate enough to be a part of, it occurred to me that with a bit of luck, I might say something of value to someone.

We were always moving—on wheels, wings, or water—but we were never away from home. Home was us, a family, sharing experiences made both possible and unavoidable by a career path that led us through six countries, five industries, and eight companies whose annual sales ranged from $50 million to $50 billion. I don't want to imply that that makes me unique, certainly not in this day of multinationals. What I believe, however, is that whatever made me different gave me a special perspective on what I saw.

I'm still not sure why or how I came by this slightly skewed point of view. Maybe it was something I inherited from my father, who came to America via Ellis Island from what is known today as Ukraine. He survived the rough-and-tumble of Produce Row. After the death of my Polish-born mother when I was fourteen, my father gave his family not only the love we needed, but instilled in us his own love of work, his integrity, and the inner strength that comes from education leavened by experience.

Then again, it could be that, though I didn't know it at the time, earning a scholarship to Princeton helped broaden my outlook. In addition to filling my father's eyes with the glow of pride, it gave me a chance to discover what it would be like to live and make friends among bright, talented, ambitious, strong-willed people who truly believe the future belongs to them. Frankly, I am content thinking it was a combination of all of the above; but what matters ultimately is that all of us play the hand dealt to us and come out of the game with something worth passing on, besides money.

Nevertheless, writing the book required lots of encouragement, help, and time from others. It took patience from some folks to get me through first-book jitters as well. I so wanted this book to be fun and worthwhile.

My heartfelt thanks go out to those who read some or all of the early drafts and gave me many great suggestions. They included John Kiker, vice president of communications at United Airlines and a great writer, Bill Hobgood and Fran Maher, senior vice presidents at United, and Lodene Spanola, my assistant, who managed to keep up with her regular duties and administrative work while helping me with the book.

I want to thank for their great suggestions and advice Jason McManus, my schoolboy friend and recently retired chief editor of Time Inc.; Laurel Cutler, my marketing guru friend; Glenda, my dear wife, my trophy wife of forty-two years; and Carol Royer.

I especially want to thank Larry Kirshbaum, my publisher at Warner Books, Rick Wolff, my editor, and Charlie Madigan, my collaborator, for their dedication to this book. And, of course, to all my teachers and mentors and bosses and colleagues, to whom I am indebted for my life's experiences, which this book tries to pass on.

CONTENTS

───────────────⭑───────────────

LESSONS FROM
THE HEART
OF AMERICAN
BUSINESS

ONE

⭐

Have the Courage to Admit You Don't Know

I don't understand airplanes and how they fly.

That probably sounds unusual coming from an executive who ran a huge airline. But I am amazed whenever I see one of United's 747s taking off. How could that much weight possibly climb so gracefully into the sky?

I don't understand computers, either.

They are plastic boxes full of mystery to me.

I could never build one, don't have the foggiest notion of what is inside of one, and, I must reluctantly admit, I am a novice at using one, although I am determined now to learn.

I never understood cars, either, at least not in the way that real car people understand cars.

You get in, turn on the engine, and drive away. That must sound like quite a confession coming from a veteran of Ford Motor Co. and then Chrysler Corp.

I have always believed it is important for an executive to understand how much he doesn't know. It's arrogant to think you know everything, and a little dangerous. It's better to recognize what you need to learn.

This is the story of my continuing education, an experience that began long before the day I walked into Ford in 1957, and, I would hope, will continue, now that I have said my formal farewells to the folks at United Airlines.

From a business perspective, at one level it's all about

good and bad bosses, the ones I have had and what they taught me about my own leadership skills and how to use them. And on another level, the story is about people who worked hard, sometimes achieving goals that seemed impossible.

At some points, it's going to seem more like a wonderful romp than a formal process. But that is how my career went for me. It was a long extension of experiences that ran all the way from the silly to the splendid, sometimes both at the same time.

I am the product of all of the places I have been, and to understand what that means, you need a road map. And for me, like most people, one has to start at the beginning.

I joined Ford Motor Co. fresh out of Princeton in 1957, back when cars had fins, no one ever thought the rest of the world would have much of an impact on the car business in America, and the thought of making $425 a month was magnetically attractive to a new grad from St. Louis.

It was a young man's game, and I was ready for whatever Ford presented. For three years, I was overseer of financial controls for Ford Latin America companies. At the Ford division of Ford North America, financial analysis was my specialty, but the job description didn't begin to cover the responsibilities I took on.

Research and development expenses, the aftermarket parts business, advertising and promotion, and labor relations were all part of that job. Then I served for two years as executive assistant to the product engineer who was responsible for compact car design. That was my baptism in the design and production of cars, an experience that brought me close to the heart of Ford's real mission.

In 1967, I was sent to Brazil to consider buying the Willys car company. After helping to negotiate the purchase from Kaiser and Renault in France, I was sent to São Paulo to be the controller. That was a challenging job that carried me deep into a different culture. We merged Willys and the smaller Ford of Brazil and developed a strong export program, all during a period of high inflation, a lesson that would prove invaluable later in my career.

I moved back to the United States in 1970 to become controller of Ford North American Truck Operations. It was a healthy time for Ford trucks, and for me, too. Our market share increased 20 percent and our profits increased by 80 percent.

I suppose it was wanderlust, and the siren call of a chance to run my own company, that carried me to France for Ford in 1972. The company had purchased Richier S.A., which made just about every machine involved in the construction business and had perfected the tower cranes that are so common on construction sites all over the world today.

It was a tough job full of unusual demands, not the least of which involved functioning as an executive in the French language, because there were few people at Richier who spoke English. I put strong financial controls in place inside a company that was bleeding money and helped slim Richier down. This job involved a complicated mix of responsibilities that carried me into government affairs, bank relations, French union negotiations, and worldwide distribution.

I moved to London to become director of all nonautomotive operations for Ford of Europe in 1974. That was another one of those titles that was just too small to describe the job. I ran power plants, constructed and managed housing for Ford workers, negotiated contracts, and even directed the renovation of a classic London guest house for Ford executives.

I was responsible for truck fleets, telecommunications systems, security services, land acquisitions, and ten thousand cars for company workers. I found a way to cut costs in that mammoth operation by 25 percent annually without damaging company operations.

In 1976, I was named president of Ford of Venezuela, an

automotive subsidiary with sales of $600 million, 150 deal-
ers, four hundred suppliers, and two assembly plants. Over
three years, sales and markets doubled for Ford, employment tripled to five thousand, and profits increased ten-
fold.

I was on the Ford fast track, having done very well at all
of my assignments.

That was when I returned a phone call that some people
thought I should have ignored.

Lee Iacocca.

He had been chased out of Ford because of his success
and aggressiveness and now headed the troubled Chrysler
Corp. Returning that call changed my career, my address,
and my life, all at the same time.

Working for Lee was like playing basketball with Michael
Jordan. He was that good. Iacocca's presence allowed
everybody on his team to play at a higher level. I think he
invented his own management style, unlike anything anyone had ever attempted.

I call it "managing by speechwriting," and it was a scary
process for anyone who wasn't aware of what Iacocca was
doing.

Being Iacocca's speechwriter was probably the worst job
at Chrysler, or at least the hardest. I have seen Lee throw
speeches back at his writers right up until the point Iacocca
climbed into the limo to head off to deliver the address.
That wasn't because he was a bad guy. The marketing people were his best editors, because they understood where
he was going along the managing by speechwriting course.

He was not a natural at speech making, but everyone
thought he was. There is an important lesson about diligence in that. I watched him build his skills even as he was
building Chrysler, thinking out loud about everything
from finance to auto design.

He would watch, talk, listen, and most important of all,
ask questions. And with every answer, he learned something new.

Lee told me once that he had learned his own lesson about priorities many years before we worked together at Chrysler.

He had asked one of his many Ford mentors for more people because he said he was overworked. His boss told him to write up a list of priorities. A month later, Lee and the boss reviewed the list. Most of his priorities had not been completed. The boss told Iacocca he didn't need more people, he just needed to proceed with the unfinished business on his list of priorities.

Lee had a downside, of course. He was just too powerful at meetings. He would overwhelm people with his own thoughts, his own process of managing by speechwriting. That was a valuable lesson for me, because I learned the importance of talking less and listening more. Putting people at ease is more than a courtesy for a CEO. It's the only way to get people to tell you the truth.

I joined Chrysler as corporate controller in 1979. It was my job to bring some financial control to a company that was going down in flames. My biggest job at Chrysler was to lobby in Washington, Canada, and five state capitals for the loan guarantees that would save the company, even as I helped Chrysler develop its business and build a plan for financial survival.

I was in charge of twenty-two task forces that covered everything from improving cash flow to obtaining financial support from four hundred banks around the world. At the same time, I coordinated negotiations aimed at winning concessions from the United Auto Workers and the Canadian Auto Workers. I was also in charge of day-to-day relations with the federal Loan Guarantee Board in Washington.

I became vice chairman of Chrysler in 1981 and took on responsibility for day-to-day operations of the $20 billion corporation. During this time, we paid off federal loan guarantees of $1.5 billion seven years before they were due, and that provided $300 million in profit to the federal government.

We also launched the Chrysler K-car and developed the minivan.

From 1985 to 1988, I was chairman of Chrysler Motors, a job that carried responsibility for all Chrysler North American automotive operations. During that time, Chrysler Motors reached peak earnings and cash flow, acquired American Motors, and had a five-year capital spending plan of $14 billion.

By 1989, I had become one-half of the two-person office of the chairman at Chrysler. Lee was the other, "bigger" half.

I shared full responsibility for operations of the company. I was directly responsible for Acustar, a $4 billion auto components business with 25,000 employees, and for Chrysler Financial Corp., a $40 billion financial services operation with 10,000 employees and four hundred offices. Chrysler Technologies, with its Gulfstream jet system, and defense contractor Electronic Systems, Inc., were also part of my watch.

I was also in charge of Chrysler International, which had sales of 100,000 vehicles annually and key partnerships with Mitsubishi and other companies in China, Italy, and Austria.

Even with all those responsibilities and all that success, it was clear to me it was time to move once again. It seemed as though Iacocca would remain chairman of Chrysler for eternity.

I had achieved what I could achieve at Chrysler.

An intriguing prospect presented itself in June 1990.

I became chairman and chief executive officer of United Employees Acquisition Corp. My job was to direct the employee buyout of United Airlines. The pilot, machinist, and flight attendant union chiefs had asked me to lead the buyout and later become the CEO of what was to be an employee-owned airline. I was intrigued by the promise of employee ownership and the changes it could bring to the world of business. We created a complicated, but effective, financial plan to buying in the $4 billion necessary for the buyout. Then the Persian Gulf War killed the financing plans.

I shifted in 1991 to Dillon Read & Co. as a managing director, where I sought acquisitions in the $100 million to $500 million range for the firm's buyout fund. I also did some advisory work, which, for the most part, I did not like.

I recall sitting with some other bankers at a meeting with Kmart chairman Joseph Antonini. We were giving him advice. It amounted to unloading everything that wasn't directly connected to Kmart's core business. I found myself sweating. It is unusual for a marathon runner to sit and sweat at a meeting. I realized at that point that I was sweating because I had absolutely no idea what I should be saying about retail sales at Kmart. It wasn't my field. I was bad at selling an idea I knew nothing about. That feeling of dishonesty made me sweat.

There was one part of my Dillon Read experience that I liked a lot. We would identify small companies that needed help to grow. I recall watching one of them grow from $80 million a year in business to $800 million a year. That part of investment banking was so compelling for me that now in retirement I am a partner with two others in an investment fund aimed at helping companies grow.

There was another shift a year later, this time to Olympia & York Developments, Ltd., as president and deputy chief executive officer in the midst of the company's liquidity crisis. We were trying to restructure $19 billion in debt with about one hundred creditors around the world to restore the company to financial health, a prospect, I quickly learned, that was doomed from the start.

After O&Y, I spent a year in what amounted to a fascinating part-time job, working on the turnaround of Tatra, the Czech Republic truck company. It was a two-year contract that required about eight weeks of my time each year, but it gave me a close look at the difficulties of making the transition from state control to market competition after the collapse of communism.

Communism had damaged the Czech Republic so deeply over four decades that Tatra simply didn't know how to compete.

In 1994, the United Airlines deal we all thought had died proved to the world that it was only resting. I had dined at that banquet before, and I was still hungry for the United job. For years, I had longed for a company of my own, a company I could lead, and this was my chance.

I became chairman and chief executive officer of United and held that job until my retirement a year ago. It was the largest employee-majority-owned company in the United States, and we set out to make it the biggest and best airline in the world.

That's quite a road map.

United fell on some hard times in the wake of my departure as its pilots and management struggled to reach a new labor contract. Thousands of flights were canceled and many of its customers became angry. I can't change that, but I remain convinced that employee ownership will prove its value over time. United's employees will solve their problems and shift their focus where it belongs, back to the customers.

From looking at my record, you might conclude: "This guy just can't seem to hold a job." But there is another way to look at it: "This guy just can't pass up a challenge."

The important part about my work record is what it represents, what I learned along the way.

As I reflected on my life's work when I was preparing this book, it struck me that I learned as much about business hiking up the sides of mountains as I learned sitting in board meetings or consulting, sometimes conspiring, with my co-workers.

There is a simple clarity to mountain climbing that I think relates directly to what happens at the office every day.

There is the mountain. Prepare yourself and go climb it.

You face something that seems overwhelming, then you measure it carefully, put your team together, attack it diligently, and succeed.

But before mapping out a strategy, I always knew that I had to do my homework. That meant educating myself on all sorts of topics.

The truth is, I was never afraid to admit that I just didn't have the foggiest notion of how something worked, or why it didn't work. It was better for me to find someone who knew, and open myself to the knowledge they had to offer.

Where did that lead?

Well, I knew nothing about airplanes, but I knew where to go at United Airlines to find out exactly what it was that put a 747 into the air. Now I know how many people it carries, how much fuel it uses, and where it fits into the grand design of our route and fleet plan, and how it can take anybody just about anyplace in the world.

I was never shy about asking about any of that.

Even though I knew nothing about the workings of computers, I knew exactly where they fit in the world of business, how they could bring efficiency, speed, and better service to our customers, how they could help us cope with the unyielding demands of change.

I know where computers fit into the profit picture of companies, what technology can accomplish and what it cannot accomplish. I can tell right away when someone who knows everything about computers doesn't understand anything about how they fit in a business.

I know that because I asked.

Early on during my years at Chrysler, I took on information technology as one of my responsibilities. It wasn't something I knew a lot about at the time, so I went to Chrysler's IT team and I asked them to tell me who knew

more about information technology than anyone else.
They came up with a list of four people, and I reached out
and invited them to discuss information technology issues
with the Chrysler team. I sat in on the meetings. I watched
Chrysler's people learning lessons from the best in the
field, and I learned right along with them.

Not knowing anything about cars at Ford was of great
value.

My quest to find out carried me into the company of engineers, mechanics, drivers, and designers who knew everything there was to know about automobiles and how to get
them from the design board into the hands of customers.

You can collect knowledge in unexpected places.

Beyond what I had learned in high school civics and college, I didn't know much about Washington.

All of that changes when your mission is to convince a
reluctant federal government that it is in the nation's interest to help save one of its most important companies,
not with handouts or grants, but by creating some conditions that would allow the company to survive.

I had a marvelous education as part of the struggle to
save Chrysler. I got to see government function from the
inside, to know how political decisions were made and what
impact they were likely to have on my company.

I was not educated in the world of high finance, but I
found out about it from people who were.

The Chrysler experience amounted to a crash course in
banking and finance at every level, from the U.S. Department of the Treasury to the last little bank that found itself
at the center trying to decide whether Chrysler's loan guarantees would be finally approved and the company saved.

Fortunately, I have never been much of a know-it-all or I
doubt I would have succeeded at any of these jobs.

If I had to label myself now at the other end of my career, I think the tag would say, "The Man Who Finds Out."

That has been my operating standard since the late 1950s.

That is what this book is all about, a career-long quest to fill in my own gaps. Knowing you have gaps is a big asset for any modern executive. People are always willing to help fill them.

I have seen plenty of folks who were convinced they had all of the answers and felt quite secure about slamming the door on knowledge and experience. That is one modern management style. I don't think it works very well, because it doesn't recognize that business has become so complicated that one mind simply can't take it all in.

Some executives brag about their golf games. I can brag about why I don't have a golf game to brag about.

My wife and I tried to learn golf in Brazil, where we were living at the time. We weren't all that interested anyway, but my attraction to the game declined even more when one of my Brazilian friends warned me never to search for missing golf balls in the rough, because there are dangerous snakes and spiders in there.

We dropped golf.

I won't have much to say about golf, then.

Mystical curses, however, I can talk about.

I was the target of a voodoo curse in Brazil, where a spider fatally bit my dog and the tile came crashing off the kitchen wall in the middle of the night.

A person with less experience might ascribe those incidents to the nature of Brazilian spiders and bad construction work. But the local interpretation was a lot more interesting and definitely made for better dinner stories.

And what does a Jewish executive say about dining in an exclusive German club in Buenos Aires with the descendants of Germans who were trapped in South America midway through World War II?

Where does sharing beer with Henry Ford II and an old

fisherman one hot afternoon on a tiny isolated island in the Caribbean fit into a business history?

Sometimes, it felt as though I were cast in the role of the lead actor in a movie.

I have camped in the jungle, climbed magnificent mountains, and slept in an igloo in the Arctic with the sled dogs howling outside. One of my neighbors was kidnapped by terrorists, and somehow that led me to ponder whether it would be proper to make sandwiches for my bodyguard.

I went on a picnic in the wilds once with some South American cowboys, big, tough men who were tickled at the fact that we had brought along one of those crank-up record players so they could listen to dance music.

None of it happened in my office, but all of it was related to my work. I got to be an executive and an adventurer, too, a great privilege and an unusual combination in modern business.

I started out in a business world that was very narrowly defined by the economics and realities of mid-century America. I am finishing my formal career in a world in which boundaries are melting away and all the old assumptions about business are facing radical revision.

If I were reading this book, I would have one big question.

If I don't know how to do any of this stuff, how did I get to the top of so many different corporations? The cynic's conclusion would be that you don't need much going for you to run a business.

Wrong!

Of course it might have been better if I had taken a different course early in life, perhaps studying engineering and getting comfortable with computers as I worked my way up in my career. But I believe I was able to compensate for this abundant lack of technical skill by using a set of talents that are of great value to anyone who plans to run a company.

I am not afraid of work.

Bless my father for giving that to me. He started his business life when he was fourteen, and was proud of it.

These days in business, there are many views about what process, what strategy, a CEO might put into place to improve his situation. I have reached a surprising conclusion about that: It's still just about hard work, and it always has been.

An executive can put any idea he wants in place and it won't go anywhere unless he understands his primary mission is to get the people all around him to embrace that notion: It's all about hard work. Sometimes, people will lose sleep, miss meals, miss birthdays, miss just about everything, all in the interest of reaching a goal.

A CEO's obligation is to create the condition that encourages that kind of work, recognizing all the time that business, cut down to its most simple definition, is all about getting people to work well together to sell a product or a service.

I wrote my own career study a little over a year ago as I was preparing to leave United Airlines, and every time I look at it I reach the same conclusion.

My story is a collection of the success stories of other folks, the people I turned to for advice and counsel over the years. You take away great value from that kind of experience, not only the knowledge, but the pleasure of getting to know people who do their jobs well.

My experience carried me from the command and control style that was so dominant in business after World War II to the era of empowerment, individual responsibility, and creativity that is emerging as a new century begins.

What worked for me will work for managers in the twenty-first century, too. Keep an open mind. Learn how to ask the right questions. Surround yourself with people who know, befriend them, and recognize the value of what they have to offer.

My roots go back to Eastern Europe, Poland, and Ukraine, to Jewish communities that disappeared during World War II. The names of those places are still on the map, Lida and Shepetovka, but the people are long since gone, most of them victims of the Holocaust.

I know that is a common sadness for American Jews, that sense that their roots were clipped off and destroyed somewhere between 1939 and 1945. So my story starts where so many American business stories start, right here at home in the United States.

I was born in 1935 and raised in St. Louis, where my father, who had arrived in the U.S. from Ukraine at age fifteen, was in the wholesale chicken business. He bought the chickens from farmers and then sold them to retail stores. I went to a wonderful public school and lived the mid-century American teenager's life, full of good buddies and girlfriends, heartbreaks, hamburgers, and sports. There was never a lot of money around, so I earned my own. Because I studied hard, got good grades, and was good at sports, I had some impressive options when the time came for college.

I chose Princeton, although I had no idea what I wanted to be. I might have been a doctor. I might have been a diplomat. I might have been a labor leader. All of those fields were attractive to me, but mostly, I was experimenting, searching for something that felt right.

I had a lot of jobs at Princeton. I was a pro at setting dining hall tables. My specialty was the left-handed fork. My friends and I had worked out a system in which each worker had a specialty and the tables were set with a regimentation and efficiency that would have impressed even the British army, with the placement of that fork being my job. Nine students cleaned and set a dining hall for 250 in twenty-four minutes flat!

For a time, I felt a little out of place, the Jewish kid from St. Louis public school surrounded by a lot of academic prep school heavyweights, some of whom came from lots of old money. But I eventually met my crew, track jocks mostly, like me, and found my way of fitting in.

Starting my junior year, I was in Princeton's Woodrow Wilson School of Public and International Affairs and later graduated from Princeton with honors.

My friends and family were surprised when I announced I would be going to work for Ford Motor in 1957. Because of Ford's background, particularly old Henry Ford's blatant anti-Semitism, the family worried whether it would be the right place for me. But I always thought prejudice was the other person's problem, and anyway, what could have been more promising than a $425 a month job in the Edsel division?

I thought it a princely sum at the time, and a job with a lot of opportunities.

The Edsel didn't last, but I did.

TWO

In the Court of the Emperor Ford

No one spends twenty-two years at Ford Motor without collecting an encyclopedia of management experiences.

"How to Be a Boss" would be one whole book in the collection.

From Henry Ford II to the people I worked with when I arrived at Ford in 1957, it adds up to more than two decades of hands-on managerial experience and a rich collection of stories that would fall under the vaguely Shakespearean heading: "How to Be. How Not to Be."

I learned a lot about the kind of boss a person needs during my years at Ford headquarters, the "Big Glass House" packed full of Ford history and, as important, Ford values.

They weren't always good values.

Too much attention was paid to covering your backside and meeting the demands of a vast bureaucracy. And too much attention was paid to climbing the management ladder. That forced everyone to deal with internal political problems.

I had two bosses who represented polar opposites in the world of management. They were both very successful by Ford's measures, but it didn't take me long to figure out which character I would want to emulate as my own career progressed.

One was Phil Caldwell, who later as CEO of Ford sponsored the first serious push for real quality improvements at a critical juncture.

He ran the truck business and I was his controller. He was all business. He would smile at the right time, but he was not into social fun.

His whole method of operation was never to make a decision until you have to because, in the meantime, you can work eighty hours a week and collect more data and ask more questions than anybody else would ask.

Therefore, you will make the best decision.

I don't think that is the way to make decisions. A lot of companies tend to study situations to death and then act long after the right time has passed. There is security in statistics. They provide a management team with the ammunition it needs to make sharp, timely decisions.

But there is also a tendency to try to use statistics to take the risk out of decision making, and that doesn't work. Understanding the balance between the need to do good research and the danger of researching an idea to death is important in a business world that moves at the speed of light.

Decision making has built-in risks. Face it and live with them.

Phil Caldwell had a peculiar management trait.

He could sit in a meeting for ten hours without going to the bathroom. We would have to sit through these sessions. It was awkward if you excused yourself to go to the bathroom. He didn't drink alcohol. He didn't drink coffee. He didn't smoke. And he didn't seem to need to pee.

He just worked.

To his credit, he made a big difference at Ford. That is a lesson in judging people for what they do, not for how they seem. He may not have been a comfortable boss (it's hard to be comfortable when you're sitting in one of those marathon meetings and your bladder is about to burst) but he was the leader who glued the word "quality" onto Ford's name, and that was important and valuable.

Even given that accomplishment, making your fellow managers comfortable with your style is one of your most important responsibilities.

A good boss has to be sensitive enough to recognize his role in the process and embrace what everyone else brings to the table.

A good boss should have a sense of fun.

Ed Molina, who was in charge of Latin American operations, was always either working or having a good time, and almost never sleeping. He accomplished as much as Phil Caldwell, but he had a great time doing it, and so did all the people around him.

He worked for Phil for a while and he couldn't stand it.

He persuaded Henry Ford II that the perfect place for Ford's Latin American headquarters was in Mexico. In fact, he would not have cared if it were anyplace but right there in Detroit.

He had to get away.

Molina was loyal to his people; he would risk his life for them. He slipped into Argentina during a time of terrorism against foreigners and organized a twenty-four-hour exodus of all of Ford's people back to the U.S.

He had a great gift. He knew how to celebrate.

He took three lawyers, very conservative types, to a club in Paris once to celebrate a big acquisition. The club was called Le Sexy (only in Paris!). I wasn't there, but I heard all about the event. They were all sitting there watching the floor show and having drinks. Ed stepped away to go to the men's room. He was bored with the show.

He stopped at the bar to have a drink. At that point, three Parisian call girls approached him. He asked if he could hire all three of them, and they said yes. Then he pointed to the lawyers at the table.

"They are going to resist," he said. "But I can assure you they are very interested."

Then he paid the call girls and left.

For a whole year, there were debates about what happened that night, whether they had successfully resisted or not. It was all part of the Molina legend at Ford. Sadly, he passed away some years ago at age sixty-three. I still miss him. (And no, I still don't know what happened that night.)

If you look at the contrast between those two bosses, the conclusion about which style works best is clear to me.

You have only so many days, weeks, and months to live and most of your time is spent working. A good boss owes it to himself and to the people around him to create an environment of excitement and fun, even while he is racking up high scores and improving the business.

At Ford during my years there, and at a lot of other companies today, I realized it is too easy to be defined by your job.

That is a mistake and it is one of the most important reasons why you always have to struggle to be a good boss. You can help people keep things in perspective.

I was completely swept up by the atmosphere at Ford.

I was representative of my generation. We were all a bunch of workaholics. We missed a lot of living because of that, our relationships with our families, our lives in the communities where we lived.

Ford had become my identity.

The atmosphere was overpowering in a lot of ways. I had a friend who came to work twenty minutes late one morning. His supervisor was standing there. He told him, "You're late." My friend told the supervisor he had worked until 2:00 A.M. the previous night.

"Okay," the supervisor said. "I'll tell you what. Tonight, work until 1:30 A.M., but make sure you come to work on time tomorrow."

I think the problem was that we just didn't have enough self-confidence. We were all Type A's and we wanted to work hard and get promoted. It was a lot like competing in sports.

Ford created that environment. People who were willing

to give up some personal parts of their lives succeeded at the office.

My jobs at Ford literally carried me all over the world and exposed me to world-class business experiences long before the phrase "world-class" worked its way into the language of business.

But I don't want to overlook what I found when I arrived at Ford, because the experience says so much about the way American companies used to be, and the way some of them still are today.

All of my Ford lessons weren't big ones.

Some fall into a category of my business life that might best be filed under: "Unusual experiences that happened along the way." Every CEO has enough of these stories to fill a filing cabinet.

They don't tell anyone how to turn a company around, how to create money from nothing, or how to solve the difficult challenges of company culture.

But they are important, too, because they help to make us aware that before we are executives, we are humans, and being human means there will be some mistakes, and some silly times, too.

Ed Molina understood that. Phil Caldwell did not.

Ford was where I first learned that, even in big, successful businesses, everything doesn't work out as planned. How about my first assignment to the Edsel division?

I was a very small cog in a huge business, a vast bureaucracy with thousands upon thousands of executives and workers. To the outside world, Ford looked like one of those paragons of American business. Steel and money went in one end, and good cars came out the other.

Building cars is a fantastic experience.

It starts with imagination, a car idea, which is transformed by engineering into a solid design product. Then car building shifts to manufacturing, where mountains of parts of every description fall into place, guided by experienced hands and a meticulously planned procedure.

There is nothing like the feeling you get when that first beautiful shiny new car you have been designing comes off the production line. It was almost like watching your baby being born. This is particularly true when you are the boss. At Ford and later at Chrysler, Lee Iacocca was in his glory when new cars were being born.

He was the new-car boss of all new-car bosses.

Car companies make a big deal of these birthing events. They make a big deal of every point along the process, too.

Companies schedule major presentations to promote new cars, or new design elements when they are ready for introduction to the public.

These days, the introduction of a new car is like a rock concert, complete with loud music, smoke machines, laser lights, and carefully scripted presentations.

It wasn't always that way.

I remember one of Lee's plans to emphasize Ford's commitment to safety before the government began mandating such things.

It was a very serious subject.

Ford made its contribution with the padded dashboard.

It doesn't seem like a big deal now, but forty years ago, if you were in an auto accident, you might hit a solid metal dashboard. Padding the dash might not seem like a gigantic leap, but it was then and undoubtedly has saved many lives.

Iacocca wanted to get his salesmen turned on about this new padded dashboard, so he scheduled a demonstration. He gathered a whole collection of salesmen in an auditorium. Up on the stage there was a table with some of the dashboard padding on it.

His plan was to climb up on a ladder and prove that this development would change the world of car safety forever.

He took a raw egg. He was going to drop it on the padding to show how effective it was. He let go of the egg and—*splat!*

It splattered all over the padding and the stage around the table.

He should have searched for a tougher egg.

I was really not in the mainstream when I started at Ford because I wanted to work in labor relations. Finance and manufacturing and engineering were the hot areas at Ford in the late 1950s. At best, I was working to support an engineering department.

But even from a distance, I was able to watch the work of a group we called the Whiz Kids. The phenomenon still exists.

Companies frequently turn to collections of young brilliants to help solve their problems, either bringing them on board or hiring them as consultants. Sometimes, an awareness of the value of the people who are already in place gets lost in that process.

It is hard to believe that something like this could happen in modern business, but Ford actually hired ten people from the U.S. Air Force as a package. As they matured and gained experience, many of them later went on to important positions in industrial America.

Bob McNamara was one of them, long before he headed into politics as secretary of defense and then moved on to the World Bank. Tex Thornton, who virtually created Litton Industries, was there, too, along with Ed Lundy, who later became financial chief of Ford Motor. They were important characters in my boss-watching years.

Initially, they were bright but not too experienced.

They were highly educated, highly energetic, and had a lot to do with the logistics of ordnance in World War II. We called them Whiz Kids because young Henry Ford II let them free to go where they wanted and question whatever they found.

It was wonderful until these young men actually got power too soon.

They awed the un-intellectuals at Ford. And they did some pretty crazy stuff in their early days.

Ford was in poor shape then.

As such, it was an ideal work environment for the young brilliants. There were plenty of problems to address. Unfortunately, there were a lot of folks at Ford who already knew how to make the place work, who had found their own ways to accomplish goals.

They were the veterans, and the Whiz Kids had no patience for them. Yes, the veterans had done some dumb things over the years, but they still had a tremendous amount of experience and a lot to offer.

The Whiz Kids would just blow right past them.

That experience left me with an important conclusion: Any successful enterprise needs bright, new people with new ideas. But it also needs the veterans who have been there and have learned from their own failures.

When I was working on the 1960 Falcon program, I had the freedom to roam. I just loved listening to the older guys reminiscing. Some of them told stories about old Henry Ford, about what a tyrant he had been.

My take from their stories: Beware of self-made, brilliant, very wealthy people. They do not believe they can make mistakes and they have very little sympathy or patience for anything, certainly not for the people who work for them.

These vets told me that by the late 1930s, Ford employees were actually hiding from old Henry Ford for fear that he would be in a bad mood and fire them on the spot for no good reason.

His goal was to try to get his grandsons into the business and trained in ways that would benefit the company.

But they were just kids. And they acted like kids.

One of the mechanics told me a story about teaching young Henry Ford II how to weld. The mechanic came into work a few days later and found that all of his tools had been welded together in his locker.

Think about that.

How do you complain at Ford Motor Co. about that kind of behavior from a teenager named Ford?

You don't.

It was part of the atmosphere inside of a company that carried its founder's name. Over time, Ford had become an empire. Even after the elder Ford had left the job, during World War II when the Defense Department convinced Henry Ford II he should take over because national security was closely tied to Ford's success, Ford Motor was an empire.

I got my first real taste of the dark side of the culture at Ford back in the 1960s.

Cultural change is one of the hot mantras of modern business. It is important, of course, but I know why it is so hard to create new cultures inside of old companies. One part of culture is a creation of the stories people tell about what they have experienced on the job.

I have been struggling with cultural problems for most of my career. We worked to rebuild the culture at United Airlines for years. Folks are always telling stories about the bad old days, and tailoring their behavior to act as though they still exist.

Distrust between management and the workers was planted years and years ago at United, but it still damages people on the job every day. A CEO can sense it when he listens to the stories people tell about their jobs. I would suggest that it has always been that way, and that the challenge of the modern CEO is to find a way to create strong, good stories that drive out the old bad ones.

I learned all about that at Ford.

What a collection of bad stories the Ford people had to tell.

Ford was still making wood propellers for the trimotor airplanes in the 1940s, long after the trimotor plane was gone. They built the propellers and sent them to a warehouse, never to be used or seen again. There was no need for the propellers, but no one in that vast company told the propeller division. That was one of the price tags attached to being so big. No one really knew enough about the place.

Every empire has an emperor.

Ford the First was the king in his era, and I think that role fell quite naturally to Henry Ford II when he took over.

He was the emperor of Ford Motor, but he never realized it.

From what he said and what he did, it was clear he never really wanted the throne. But he couldn't help it. He inadvertently created whole divisions of yes-men around him. No one would dare tell him something he didn't want to hear. Some punishment would follow if you broke that rule. Smart people do that once or twice and never do it again.

This problem was not unique to Ford. And it is not unique to the 1950s, either. Despots who surround themselves with people who can only say yes run modern companies. That makes it difficult to talk honestly about problems, and particularly difficult to solve them.

Ford suffered because of it.

Energy and attention were constantly focused on what Henry Ford II wanted, or worse, on what people thought Henry Ford II wanted. This remains a common challenge in modern management and it is why honest, candid internal communication is so important.

A CEO doesn't need a whole army of subordinates running around trying to guess what he wants, but that was standard procedure at Ford.

I have seen this kind of problem, the CEO as emperor, play out on many stages. Later in my career, when I was running that truck company in the Czech Republic, I saw how communism had taken all the initiative out of people.

As strange as it might sound, I remember sitting there in Prague thinking, My Lord, some of this kind of behavior comes straight from the world of Ford of the 1950s and 1960s.

Fundamentally, like a lot of us at Ford, Henry Ford II didn't have self-confidence, which made him the opposite of his grandfather.

He had a lot of wonderful qualities, but he also had a characteristic that I have seen in folks who have inherited extraordinary wealth.

They are afraid someone is going to take their money, and ultimately their power, away from them.

That paranoia has always puzzled me.

I saw Henry Ford II drive good people out of the company because he was afraid they were coming too close to his power.

Iacocca was only one of the big names forced out because he came too close to the throne. Iacocca got a lot of publicity after the Mustang introduction and he later opened his own channels of communication with some board members.

That was the kiss of death at Ford and before Iacocca knew what hit him, he was out the door. He spent his last days sitting at a little desk in a parts depot someplace. It was unfair and ugly, the price attached to making Henry Ford II worried.

Ford's paranoia was on display much of the time.

Why would a guy in that position with all the power that no one was ever going to take away feel the need to say at least once a week, "Let me remind you whose name is on the building!"

The damage spread all over the business.

In California, the car-buying public was turning to smaller cars, and the Japanese had found a way to tap that potential market.

But Henry Ford II had no time for small cars.

If the Japanese wanted to build them, let them. There

was one visionary in the company, Hal Sperlich, who knew Henry Ford II was wrong. I worked for him at Ford, and he worked for me later at Chrysler.

He was an original—a genuine out-of-the-box thinker. Nine out of ten ideas would be just plain nuts, but that one idea in the batch was brilliant and right on.

From his experience with the Falcon and the Mustang, Sperlich knew Ford just had to come up with a product that would compete with small Japanese cars.

Everyone was laughing about it because Henry II liked to hear the laughs—tinny little cars, what did the Japanese know?

Henry Ford's position on small cars was clear to everyone:

"Small cars. Small profits. Forget it."

But Hal was a battering ram. He just kept coming back. Looking back, I think his tenacity became a challenge to Henry II's unilateral view of power. There was no way Ford Motor was going to do small cars at that point, even though it should have.

In the end, Hal Sperlich got fired for it, a victim, in a way, of the environment of fear that management had created in that era at Ford.

There are two valuable lessons here:

The first is that there is sometimes a high price attached to fighting for what you believe in. It always raised questions in my mind about the real objective. Was it to develop a good small car, or was it about personalities? Martyrdom obviously has its place in religious history, but there is not much justification for it in business.

I am not advocating meekness in the face of resistance. I am not that way myself and I don't believe it has any place in modern management. But I would pose a question: Who suffers the most when an idea is rejected because someone is fired for being too aggressive?

Everyone with any experience has seen these situations play out.

Someone has a good idea that is not widely embraced. He tries to get it implemented and hits a brick wall. He becomes embittered and announces, in a way everyone will understand: "Screw this! I'm outta here."

In most cases, the individual is punishing himself a lot more than he is punishing the corporation that doesn't see things his way.

The second lesson, probably more important and practical, is that the goal must never be to pound your chest and say, "That's my brilliant idea that went down in flames and took me with it."

The challenge, the goal—the mountain the modern executive has to climb—is getting the idea implemented.

If you are dealing with a man like Henry Ford II, then you had better figure out how to make him think *your* idea was *his* brilliant idea. I know that doesn't sound very direct, but you have to decide what the real goal is in business. If getting the idea accomplished means giving up the credit, you have to decide which is more important.

Early on, when I was working in finance, I found myself working late on a plan that was to be presented at a meeting the next day. I called my wife, Glenda, and told her I would not be able to go out to dinner.

She asked me why.

"I have an idea, I told it to my boss, and tomorrow morning there is going to be a big meeting and I have to get this idea to a senior vice president who is going to be at the meeting. I have to write a letter for my boss to sign and send along to his boss. I have to write a second letter for this boss to sign and send to the third level, and another letter to the boss at the fourth level, and by the time I write that letter number four, that will be the man who goes to the meeting. And the last letter, of course, has to be on blue paper, not white paper, because it is being signed by a vice president, and heaven forbid a vice president should be sending a letter on mere white paper."

There was a pause.

"Honey," Glenda said. "Whose idea is it?"

"It's mine."

"And who is going to the meeting tomorrow?"

I named the senior vice president.

"Why don't you just pick up the phone, tell him your idea, and then we can go to dinner?"

And I said, "Honey, you just don't understand."

But she did. She understood perfectly.

I was the one who didn't understand. I was buying into one of the worst features of modern business, the bureaucracy trap. Glenda's would have been a lot better way to convince that vice president this was a good idea and let him carry it to the big meeting next morning. The message would have been unfiltered and clear. That would have been much more effective. Instead, I was drawn into the nonsense of hierarchy and petty status symbols.

I watched that process for years at Ford and how it chewed up ideas and wasted resources. It carried everyone from the real objective, getting good ideas implemented promptly, and put them into a world in which meeting the demands of the bureaucracy became all consuming and an end in itself.

Based on that kind of experience, I think most of the efforts to slash away at bureaucracy in the 1980s were really wise. Bureaucracy and flexibility are the oil and water of management. They just don't mix.

You have to be ruthless in cutting levels of management and in insisting that each manager have many, many people reporting directly to him or her, with fewer levels, more delegating, faster decisions, clear communications. Even in flat organizations, bureaucratic systems can be debilitating.

Pick a person to be champion of a cumbersome paper system and tell everyone you want to take about half of the cost and time out of it.

Undermine silos! That was one of the big lessons from the Ford years. Don't let communication run up and down silos. Let employees create informal networks that let people work across those silos.

There is no better example of how damaging this process is than approval systems for capital spending.

The typical system in a big company is awful.

A piece of paper—a capital spending project—finally lands on a senior manager's desk. There are fifteen signatures on the paper. That means that one piece of paper had to go in line, in sequence, to fifteen different people. It took three days to a week for each. Some had questions. Some others had the same questions. Some had no questions.

It can take months. If the assumption is that the job of a company, particularly a service company, is to respond quickly to the needs of its customers, then a procedure like that is silly.

I have a solution.

Limit the number of signatures to five. That is plenty of review. Ten other people can get a copy at some point. Then set deadlines. The first person who has the idea writes it up, sends it to the five for approval, all at the same time. Each has ten days to sign on or reject, or their silence means approval.

The underlying message is simple.

The person who comes up with the proposal takes a lot more responsibility, because we are saying, "Pal, you better be right about this." There is also a lot more accountability in a structure that allows you to identify the source of an idea. You are not spreading blame, or credit, across fifteen managers and vice presidents.

At Ford, I found that the people created their own way to work despite the atmosphere and the bureaucracy. It became clear to me that if the company depended on the formal system and bureaucracy it couldn't function. Ford would have stopped moving. It would have atrophied.

Ford worked because I wasn't the only Jerry Greenwald on the scene. It worked because there were a lot of people around who, like me, viewed filling vacuums and working around the system as their chief job description. When the system caused everything to freeze, someone would pop up and say, "Well, I have this thought. Here is a way we can get this done."

We had a problem when I was at Ford in Brazil. It was basically a bureaucracy problem that anyone in business will understand immediately.

We were working on our business plans for the coming year, and paperwork was just flying back and forth between Ford's Detroit headquarters in the United States and Brazil. Remember, in 1968, there were no faxes, no Internet, poor phones. Paperwork was literally flying back and forth, but it might just as well have been crawling—talk about snail mail!

It was a pretty stupid process. Headquarters wanted to know how many cars would be sold by the car industry in Brazil during the next three years, as if anyone could possibly know that. Headquarters wanted to know what share of each car market segment, small, midsize, large, Ford Brazil would achieve.

Believe me, if I had followed that system I would still be in Brazil, processing paper and answering questions.

I went to my boss. I told him I wanted to get on an airplane and go to Detroit. There were four different departments at headquarters all asking similar questions. They had no sense of a deadline or of the need to work together.

"I'll just go up there and go to each of the four departments and get them to sign off," I suggested.

"Okay," he said. "Do it."

It sounds like a day's work, doesn't it?

It took ten days. I just wore them down intellectually and physically. I knew much more about any of the issues than they did. Finally, they were defenseless. They just let me loose and we all got on with plans for Ford Brazil.

I have thought about that experience many times over the years. I am much more clearly focused on the business part of business these days. I had a simple edict at United. I wanted to create a system that worked so efficiently that people didn't need to work around it or fill vacuums for the company to get something accomplished.

If the system doesn't meet that test, if it isn't simple and effective, then it shouldn't be there.

Even as I was thinking back to this old Ford experience, I was visiting United's folks at Dulles International Airport outside Washington, D.C. One of our employees cornered me and asked me to take a tour of the Red Carpet Club with her.

"You see, those chairs are tattered," she said.

"Well, yes, what's going on?" I replied.

"It's been that way for two years. We have submitted proposals four times to headquarters. Nothing."

All of this bureaucracy is well meaning, of course; that's the worst of it. No one deliberately wants to slow anything down. I looked into it.

There is a group at United headquarters that is responsible for the planning and modernization of the Red Carpet Clubs all over the world. They don't have enough money to do everything all at once, so they have to set priorities.

I talked to the team responsible for the clubs.

I told them I wasn't saying that the chairs at the Red Carpet Club in Dulles should have been fixed two years ago, but I was saying that their system was awful.

The Dulles folks had applied four different times over two years for the money to fix the chairs.

In retrospect, I knew what happened.

Somebody at headquarters created the perfect orderly process that just didn't work.

I finally got my chance to work in labor relations at Ford in 1958.

This was a strong lesson in the nature of culture inside big companies.

The atmosphere had been poisoned by what labor historians call "The Battle of the Overpass." It happened on May 26, 1937. Walter Reuther, the president of United Auto Workers local 174, and some local members showed up at Ford's massive River Rouge plant to pass out leaflets urging unionization.

Reuther and three other union activists were severely beaten by a collection of goons Ford had hired as a security force.

Years later, even I paid a price.

There was a labor relations research group at headquarters that conducted all the preplanning for labor contracts. I was a candidate to go into that group.

Because of the history of labor strife at Ford, anyone headed for the planning group in those days was intensively investigated.

It wasn't perfunctory.

I got to read my investigative file later.

If I were locked up for two days to remember everything I could about myself, I could not have remembered half of what I found in the report. The Ford investigators went to talk to my grade school teachers! They discovered I was living with some distant cousins in Detroit. I had a room in their house. The husband worked for an RCA plant and was a member of the United Auto Workers.

That was all the Ford investigators needed to hear.

They would not let me come into that research department.

I did, however, get my chance to work in labor relations in the early 1960s.

Right away, I ran into an unusual situation. There was a huge Ford complex at River Rouge, a creation of Henry Ford I, who wanted total vertical integration in car manufacturing, including making his own tires.

Each plant in the complex had its own local union structure. If someone was laid off, they could only come back to that plant when the plant was rehiring based on seniority.

Someone could get laid off from the foundry with twenty years of seniority, but younger folks might be working with only two years of seniority at the assembly plant.

I showed up on the scene just after Ford and the United Auto Workers had changed the labor contract to give laid-off workers what were known as bumping rights. It carried me right into the heart of a gender issue long before anyone even knew what gender issues were.

There were a lot of forty-five-year-old women who had been laid off from some of the Rouge plants. They were the Rosie the Riveters left over from World War II. But under the new contract, they were able to bump young men in other plants who had been working for two or three years.

The whole chatter in the union was, "What the hell is this? These women are second breadwinners and they are going to take away jobs from these young men who are just starting their families?"

We tried to play it straight. The union said they had not anticipated this problem and realized they were in for a big headache.

The union's idea was that the women couldn't bump the young male workers. The women had to qualify for the jobs they wanted. So it would be easy for a management person to just say, "You don't qualify." These women picketed their own union offices! The fact was they were not second breadwinners in many cases. They needed the money.

My assignment was to help handle some of the bumping cases. It was very early boss training for me. I got a close look not only at the gender issues, but at racial issues, too.

The union local was made up of some African-Americans and some Caucasians. Some of the people coming in to bump were African-Americans, and they were going after jobs held by Caucasians. I was getting all kinds of hints about overlooking things and disqualifying African-Americans.

One particular case sticks in my mind.

I sent an African-American man to be tested for a job

that had been held by a Caucasian who had been removed because he didn't have the seniority. Three hours after the African-American got there, the foreman sent him away, saying he could not do the job.

I saw through it.

I went down to the foreman, told him he was going to have trouble—not from me, but from other African-Americans—with this case. I asked him to give the man a day and a half on the job before the foreman made his decision. The foreman was kind of meek, so he agreed.

I was heading back to my desk when the superintendent, a big, tough guy, pulled the foreman aside and asked him what had happened. I will never forget the moment. I was stepping over the conveyer line going back to where I worked when I heard this booming voice.

"Hey pretty boy, get over here!"

It was like I was on stage. All the spotlights were on me. I was the only guy wearing a tie within miles. I could feel the eyes of the three hundred people who were within earshot. I can still feel it. I did what I was told!

I learned some new language.

He told me, "You don't tell us line guys what to do."

I told him I thought we were going to end up with more trouble than we knew how to handle. But he wouldn't agree with me. The best I could do was to tell him, "Well, think about it."

I went back to my office. About ninety minutes later, I heard from the superintendent. He said, "Aw, screw it. We'll give him the chance."

It only took a few of those experiences to make me rethink my move into labor relations.

I was being drawn gradually toward finance at Ford, the pathway that would define the rest of my career there.

It wasn't part of any plan, it was just happening.

I had one great assignment as part of that process, one

that taught me a great lesson about looking outside your own corporation for practices that work.

Ford had enormous costs for facilities, testing, and personnel within the engineering organization. They had some ten thousand engineers and support people, and they had no idea how to control the expenses for that group and not undermine the basic engineering missions.

The Ford people told me to go out and benchmark. It was as if I had been hired as a consultant. They gave me three months. I could go wherever I wanted to go, do whatever I had to do, but I had to come back with an answer.

I went to Goodrich and Boeing and a couple of other companies. The people welcomed me, but it didn't take long for me to run into an old problem at Boeing. I sensed a bit of coldness. I was having a drink with one of the Boeing old-timers when he confessed and told me about the problem.

Even though it was 1960, there was still bad blood between Boeing and Ford over an issue from the Korean War. Boeing had subcontracted the wings of a military airplane to a Ford facility that had converted from car production to wing production.

Halfway into this project, Ford realized that the profits on their subcontract with Boeing were enormous and out of line. If the government found out, Ford would be in for criticism. That government criticism could hurt the company's car sales.

So, Ford sent a crew to Boeing and announced it wanted to give some of the money back.

Boeing said, "Don't talk about it." If the government got word that Boeing was lax in subcontracting, it would get angry with Boeing.

There was a big fight about this issue. Ford finally threatened that if Boeing didn't take the money back, Ford would return it directly to the federal government. And that is exactly what happened, much to Boeing's embarrassment.

That created a long-lasting rift between the companies.

*   *   *

I had never seen a computer before. As part of my investigation at Boeing, I got to look at this marvelous machine that created stacks and stacks of paper full of answers to any question you might want to ask about engineering costs.

"Does it help you reduce costs?" I asked.

They looked at me as though I were from Mars.

"The cost to create all this paper is in the overhead that we make a profit on," they said. "And we can answer any government inspector's questions."

I hope, I pray, government contracting has evolved since the early 1960s.

I thought, "I don't think this will do much good at Ford."

In the end, I came up with a plan that helped address the question of engineering costs at Ford.

That experience was my entrée into the world of finance.

I got involved in all kinds of financial work. I got to help control advertising costs. I was part of what we viewed as mission impossible, controlling the expenses of the Ford racing program.

It was a great assignment. I went to all of the races. I helped resolve arguments about who was going to get spark plug royalty rights. I got to watch all the beautiful young women who buzzed around racecar drivers like honeybees.

I got to handle unusual financial problems.

I got a bill once for women's dresses, lots of them. I asked the manager to explain that.

Someone believed that women would make better Mobil Economy Run drivers because they could drive a little slower and use less gasoline. Each night, the manager told me, we end up in a different town and he thought it would be nice if all the women had beautiful uniforms.

Well, why not!

I don't think Henry Ford II had any idea about the amount of expense he created when he announced: "I want to win Le Mans!"

Well, $30 million later, Ford did win that race.

It was a lesson in the nature of ambitious people.

Looking back on my Ford years, I think I made some personal tradeoffs that, to this day, I am not comfortable with. That was all part of that Type A personality that was so valuable in the 1950s at Ford.

It took me a long time to learn the lesson, but I finally did get smart about it. You can only push people so far. If you push them to the point at which you cause problems in their personal lives, you have stepped over the line.

I had a conversation with a young executive a little while ago about this same issue.

He told me his wife didn't understand that part of his job was to go out at night with customers. I asked him what he would be doing for the next three nights. He told me he would be going out with customers.

"Well, if I were in your shoes, I would cancel two of those three evenings and go home," I said.

I was trying to tell him that I recognized that work is important, but that it isn't always all-consuming important. In my view, he was swept up in the chase. He wasn't stepping back and thinking about the balance of life.

He reminded me a lot of myself at that age.

★

THREE

We'll Always Have Paris: Around the World for Ford

The world and the United States work on different agendas, the first and most important management lesson from my world traveler years.

By the time I finished working at Ford, I had held executive positions in Brazil, France, England, and Venezuela. And those jobs gave me work experiences in ten other countries.

What did I learn?

The first message is that education doesn't stop at the office. At the time, what you are learning might not make much sense, but it could hold valuable lessons for later.

Still, you go on learning.

In one experience alone, I learned why you might need to keep a drill press on hand, why Inspector Clouseau might have been a character from real life, and what it is like to face a collection of tough French cops with big guns when you are literally sitting on a couple of hundred million dollars in bearer stock, which is as good as money.

That was all part of a Ford disaster in which I played a central role, the decision in 1972 to purchase Richier S.A., a mess of a company that made everything from tower cranes to highway paving equipment.

But I will tell you more about Richier and why it was such a bad deal later.

First, you have to hear about the stock that sealed the

contract and the wacky process of actually buying the company.

J.P. Morgan, the banker for the Ford-Richier deal, had accumulated thousands of shares of bearer stock. The previous stockholders would give the shares to Morgan, and the bank would give them Ford's money.

Morgan had no more room in its Paris vault and wanted to transfer all of those shares, hundreds of thousands of them, to Ford.

I was Ford's man on the scene. I wanted to do everything right, and the first item on the agenda was taking good care of all of those shares.

I told our treasurer that we would take them. But he wanted to know where we would put them. They were just as negotiable as cash and they had to be in a secure place.

He said we had a vault in Paris, but we couldn't put these shares in our vault because the vault wasn't insured.

So, insure the vault!

No, he said, the underwriters won't insure the vault because it isn't theft-proof. It has four thick steel walls, but a very thin floor and a very thin ceiling.

I talked to Morgan. They had $165 million in bearer shares sitting in their vault and we had to take them within a few days. We had nowhere to put them. I told the bank to keep them until we solved the problem, but they wouldn't. The bank had more business coming in and no room.

It was time to call Ford in Detroit.

There was a simple solution, Detroit said.

Just take the shares and punch a hole in them.

In the official books, register that they have been canceled and print up one new stock certificate for all the shares in the name of Ford Motor Co.

I said okay.

Then I told the treasurer we had to be careful when Morgan delivered these shares to us, because they were just like cash until they had been punched. I had visions of bandits in black masks and berets running off with our money.

We'll hire a guard to watch the vault while we are punching holes in the shares, I said. That should protect us.

We asked Morgan to deliver those shares discreetly. Please.

J.P. Morgan showed up at 3:00 P.M. Friday in full view of all the passers-by with a Brinks truck and all these big guys with guns.

They had many packages tied with ropes. They looked like old newspapers.

I was getting nervous.

I said I wanted to meet the guard, just in case.

He looked to be about ninety years old. He had no gun.

I talked to the treasurer. He said the security company sent the old character because they didn't have enough notice, and he didn't have a gun because French law prohibited it. There was a fear these people might hurt themselves if they carried weapons.

"Oh man," I said. "We had better get to punching holes now."

We spent an hour at it before the treasurer noted that he had calculated how long it would take to punch holes in each of 365,000 shares of stock.

It would take us three weeks.

"We can't do it this way," I said.

We decided to leave late Friday and trust in our guard.

Then we decided to buy a drill press. Off we went hunting in the hardware stores of Paris on Saturday morning for a drill press.

With drill press in hand, my folks were in the vault punching holes. It was getting very hot. They looked for a window to get some fresh air. They took a ladder from the vault, opened a high window, and left the ladder sitting there, to be picked up later.

In the meantime, there was a change of guards.

The ninety-year-old guard went home. His father showed up to replace him. He knew nothing about anything.

Put yourself in this old man's position.

You hear noises inside a vault. You see a ladder at the window.

Voilà! It must be thieves. You call the police.

These very tough French gendarmes showed up. They had great big pistols. They were pointing them at my fellows in the vault, who were trying to explain why they were supposed to be ruining these shares of stock.

It took two hours to straighten it out. I kept looking for Inspector Clouseau to show up.

"So, do you have a leesanze for zees ladder here?" he might ask. Meanwhile, thieves would be running off with our stock.

By Saturday night, we had punched all the shares and we were safe.

Even closing the deal to buy Richier was strange.

We were to have a closing at J.P. Morgan on a Friday afternoon.

We would give them the money and they would transfer all those shares of stock. We got a very strange call from Ford in Detroit saying there was a problem, some last-minute audit discrepancies. It would take the weekend to figure it all out, Ford said, so just delay the closing.

So we went to our Paris lawyer, Charlie Torem, an outside attorney with a colorful past. He was tall, sophisticated, funny, and very well connected.

An American who went to Paris on an assignment, he had simply decided to stay. His greatest claim to fame was a phone call he received at 2:00 A.M. from a hotel manager in a panic.

The caller asked the attorney if he handled divorce cases. The attorney paused and said, "Well, yes."

The hotel manager told him Aly Khan, one of the world's wealthiest men at the time, was really angry with his wife and wanted a divorce.

Mrs. Aly Khan? That was Rita Hayworth.

I told our lawyer that Ford wanted to delay the closing. He said there were problems, that we were legally bound.

A complicated set of telephone calls ensued, this in the era before the speakerphone or conference call. Our attorney was working two telephones, almost choking himself with the cords.

We were running out of time.

It was almost 5:00 P.M. and we were sitting in an office on the Champs-Élysées, the busiest time on the busiest street in Paris.

Richier's lawyer told him, "Well, I have listened to all of your excuses. You are legally bound to complete the closing. I am hanging up the telephone and going to J.P. Morgan and I expect you to be there." *Bang.* You could hear it when the Richier attorney slammed down the phone.

I looked at my lawyer and he looked at me.

"What now?"

"We go to the bank!"

Like wild crazies, the two of us rushed down the steps and out into the middle of the Champs-Élysées to flag down a taxi. We made it to the bank before closing, but the Richier lawyer wasn't there. We waited and waited. It was 6:00 P.M. and he still had not arrived. A crucial business transaction was hanging on this closing.

We didn't want it to happen because Ford Detroit wasn't ready yet, but we thought we were stuck.

The banker looked at us and said in his nice French way, "We will sign the papers, but there will not be a transfer of shares or money because our vault closes at 6:00 P.M. automatically and will not be available to us until Monday."

The lawyer and I looked at each other.

I burst out laughing and the lawyer burst out laughing.

"Well," I told the banker. "Without the money and without the shares, we won't be signing anything. We'll see you Monday."

And that's when we closed the deal, on Monday, after the Ford audit had cleared.

That's how France was.

And that was how working as an executive in the non-U.S. world was.

It takes a brief return to the road map to explain what in the world I was doing (and where I was doing it) at Ford between 1967 and 1979, when I left to join Lee Iacocca at Chrysler. I worked in Detroit from 1957 to 1967, climbing that Ford ladder and learning all the way up.

Then I went to Brazil from 1967 to 1970, shifted back to Detroit until 1972, moved to Paris to try to salvage Richier from 1972 to 1974, moved to London to head Ford's nonautomotive operations from 1974 to 1976, and then ran Ford of Venezuela from 1976 to 1979.

I got my first real sense of how the United States looks to the rest of the world when I moved to Brazil to work for Ford's Latin American division in 1967. I was controller of Ford of Brazil for three years.

This was quite a shift, moving from my experience at Ford in Detroit into other cultures and other ways of doing business.

Detroit was all about working in the kingdom of the Emperor Ford. But the world had a different set of opportunities, and experiences, to offer.

As ironic as it might sound, I believe I had to leave the United States to get a real taste of business freedom, and the obligations and responsibilities that it carries.

It is important, particularly for American businesspeople moving out into a world economy, to recognize that what works in the United States will not necessarily work elsewhere.

Culture plays a deciding role inside companies. But it plays an even bigger role in other countries. The kind of cookie-cutter management style that is so common in American businesses may have little or no value in a foreign country.

In fact, it could well be damaging. Overlayering of management was a common business practice in the United States after World War II, and it translated into tremendous inefficiency and created huge bureaucracies when that style was applied in Europe.

Rule books that don't work very well in America don't work at all overseas. A key manager in a foreign country must react creatively to unusual situations, and he needs the confidence and the autonomy to do that.

It is important to recognize how you are viewed from a distance.

My world business adventure was the first point in my life at which I had a sense of how America, and Americans, look to people in other countries.

There is a groundswell of concern in other countries related to U.S. power and how it is to be applied. Free trade is wonderful, but we cannot tell other countries what their minimum wage should be. International Monetary Fund tough medicine works, but it needs better explanation if it is to be accepted.

American assumptions about life and work don't travel well.

Relocate to Latin America, or France, or England, and you learn right away that you have moved a long way from the Type A personalities who often do so well at corporate headquarters back home. Some of that Type A behavior is very valuable, and some of it doesn't fit at all.

I could never have imagined, for example, a collection of festive workers moving on Henry Ford II with a plan to throw him in a swimming pool in Detroit.

But we rescued Henry from what would have been a very damp evening in Rio, during carnival. It wasn't an exceptional event, either. Sooner or later, everyone was expected to end up in a swimming pool during carnival.

The tradition was to follow a band along Copacabana Beach, turn in at a hotel, and then, for anyone close enough, to toss them into the hotel swimming pool.

Henry Ford II came that close! We saved him at the last minute.

My initial Brazilian assignment was to look closely at the prospect of purchasing Willys from Kaiser and Renault. We did that, then merged it with the smaller Ford of Brazil. We installed financial controls and, in just one year, developed substantial export programs from Brazil for Ford.

Doing business in Brazil was not at all like doing business in the United States. The biggest challenge was wrestling with runaway inflation.

The cultural change was huge.

My friends worried about my plan to take the family to Brazil.

Wasn't I concerned about the violence, which was a staple in daily media reporting about Latin America? Wasn't I afraid of kidnapping?

What about terrorism?

Those questions generally come from people who haven't been *there*. What I found is that a different set of questions comes from people who haven't been *here*.

In Brazil, my friends were very worried about my trips back to the United States.

Wasn't I afraid to go back to a country where Dr. Martin Luther King, Jr., and Robert F. Kennedy had been slain? Wasn't I worried about street violence and all the crime reports that had come to define the United States for so many people in other countries?

One of my Brazilian friends told me he would never be a U.S. citizen.

I asked him why. This was during the Vietnam War. He said he had three sons, and as Brazilians, they were not likely to go to war.

That thought stuck with me for the rest of my life, because I have sons, too. I recognize military service as a part of the price of being a citizen of a world power, but I am fortunate that my own sons came of age when the United States was at peace.

I picked up a lot of important business experience in my jobs in foreign countries. But I think the most valuable lessons learned have as much to do with life as they have to do with work.

Americans, Koreans, and Japanese can teach the rest of the world how to work.

They are so focused and so industrious that they present the most valuable role models if you measure life in terms of business productivity.

But if you want a role model for the delight of living, turn to the Brazilians and the French.

They have a very simple and effective formula: Work hard. Play hard.

Don't get the two mixed up.

At carnival time in Brazil, I found, it was impossible to get the Brazilians to focus on work. I have never before or since seen human beings drunk on music, literally drunk on music, not on alcohol. We went to carnival with a friend and he was listening to the music of a street band that was wandering the streets of Rio.

He decided to follow the band.

We didn't see him for a day and a half.

He just kind of kept going, as though he were following the Pied Piper.

Trying to resist this part of the culture is foolish. The challenge for the American businessperson is to build his operation around it, recognizing that no one is going to get anything done at carnival time. You only demoralize everyone and make them sour about their work if you get in the way of their playtime.

Adjust to it.

We also take it for granted that because we are a results-oriented society, the rest of the world should be, too.

But it is not.

I had a conversation with a British businessman about this. He was working for a U.S. company at the time. He thought Americans were a breath of fresh air. When they had a problem, they would sit at a table and discuss how they were going to solve it.

"In Britain," he said, "we sit at a table and talk about everything but solving the problem."

Before that conversation, it had never occurred to me that problem solving by consensus was an American trait, but it is. That means that if you are doing business in England and a problem comes up, you had better know how to present it and discuss it in ways that your English friends will respond to.

Scaring people with too much aggression just freezes them in place.

I believe the French have found the best balance between work and play. They work long hours between Monday and Friday, but, by gosh, you had better make clear to them that it is World War III if you want them to stay late on Friday or work Saturday or Sunday. That is their time.

Forget about August. It is hopeless. They will all be away.

To me, that is the right balance.

Work hard and play hard.

I'm telling you about these conclusions up front because they will help you understand the rest of the story, and why it is so important to recognize other cultures if your career carries you outside the United States.

That way, instead of saying to yourself, "Gee, why would they do that?" You can say, "Of course! It's the Brazilian way of doing it!"

I had a wonderful time working for Ford in Brazil. But I was still a Ford man, and my goal was to sell as many big cars as I could. I had convinced a Brazilian friend that he should consider buying a big Ford. He argued that a Ford just wouldn't hold up because he had a fazenda, a ranch, in the interior and drove there every weekend.

I told him I was convinced the Ford would do the job. I suggested he invite me for a weekend. I would drive my Ford to his ranch, and if it held up, he would buy the car.

The ranch was a hundred miles inland from São Paulo, and it was as if a hundred years fell away the moment we crossed over into the next state, Mato Grosso, Big Savannah.

The roads were all dirt, with really big potholes. They were so deep that my fenders got dented. We found the ranch.

The car was fixed and the rancher later bought a Ford, so that plan worked, but not without some adventure first.

The first thing my friend did was strap on his pistol.

"What are you doing that for?" I asked him.

"Well, wait until you meet the ranch hands," he said.

Sure enough, these were some of the most primitive people I had ever met. They had never been to school. Their whole life was cattle, prostitutes, and alcohol.

If they liked you, there wasn't anything they wouldn't do for you.

If they didn't like you, they might just kill you.

They wouldn't think twice about it.

The cowboys were having a big celebration. They had killed a steer and they were barbecuing it. My friend brought an old-fashioned record player along. It was one of those old crank-up 78s. They all stood around it, watching it.

I thought they were listening to the music. But they were really just watching it turn. They had never seen one. They were fascinated.

We were with Ford in Brazil for three years, but we viewed the job as a jumping-off point to visit the rest of the continent. Glenda and I took the family just about everywhere. We drove from São Paulo all the way down to Punta del Este, just south of Montevideo. We went north to La Paz, Bolivia, with the family as well.

I think this is a universal experience for American businesspeople. When they know they are only going to be staying in a country for three years, they try to make the most of it.

After three years, I was too ambitious to really enjoy it. I thought it was time to move on, to get back to Ford in Detroit and work on my career. Glenda didn't want to go, because Brazil had been wonderful for her.

We had only one angry moment. We went back to Detroit in January in a blizzard. We didn't even have coats for the kids.

She looked at me and said, "Don't ever do this to me again."

It wasn't just the weather.

That is a lesson, too, for the American businessperson who would live in a foreign country. I think a lot of it had to do with the fact that living in Brazil for three years, we idealized life in the U.S. Our assumption was that the phones always worked and you could get things done. The cottage cheese is good and the hot dogs are wonderful.

But we had forgotten that life isn't perfect anywhere.

It was a shock to come back and find it wasn't so easy to buy a house, and it wasn't so easy to find a carpenter to come out immediately when you needed some help.

It was January of 1970.

I came back to Detroit from Brazil with essential experience that would be very valuable in the coming battle. Inflation was starting to heat up in the U.S., and I knew all about running a business during inflationary times.

In Brazil, inflation had been running at 30 percent a year. We knew that we had to raise our car and truck prices every month just to keep up. And we had to be very careful about our costs, even though it was difficult to understand what those costs were going to be because prices were changing—climbing so quickly.

It's hard for most American businesspeople to connect with the idea of working in inflationary times these days. In America 2000, it simply isn't a problem.

But here is a simple point to clarify what can happen.

If you don't pay close attention to costs during times of inflation, and don't build those growing costs into the price of your product, then you will lose money very quickly on everything you sell.

I showed up in the United States just as inflation was starting, and it became clear almost immediately that the people at Ford's North American Truck Operations, where I was the new controller, didn't know how to handle it.

I was shocked when I found that our folks were thinking in such simplistic terms about inflation.

"Maybe we can raise prices about $25. Or maybe $35."

I told them they just didn't get it. They should be looking at the percentage increase in costs because of inflation. Once they had calculated that figure, they should raise prices by at least that same percent and forget about how many dollars were involved.

"You have to keep up," I said, "or you are going to get eaten."

It took me a year to get the folks at Ford truck to understand that. It seems so simple, but they had come from a noninflationary world.

It is easy to forget those lessons in flush times of low inflation. My fear is that if inflation returns to the U.S., we will have to learn how to do business all over again.

I had three bosses at the Ford truck division within two years. One of them was Phil Caldwell, the ten-hour-meeting man with the big bladder. He was so deliberate that changes were glacial. Then there was Don Petersen, brilliant but stayed about only nine months.

Then Hal Sperlich came in, and he was wonderful.

But I was a little out of place working as controller in the truck division.

I had not gone to Harvard Business School. My background was in labor and economics.

Ford was big and its financial people were highly trained and specialized. It was simply the wrong fit.

There was another problem, too. Brazil had given me a taste of being out in the world, and I loved it. I was a generalist in Brazil, far from headquarters, dealing with problems on the ground without much supervision. I liked that feeling so much that I decided I wanted to be back out in the world again.

I raised my hand and said, "The next foreign assignment, I want to be considered."

Paris.

It was a measure of the strangeness of Ford Motor Co.
that they thought they would actually have to convince us
to move to Paris!

A company has to lay on the perks and work hard to convince people to move to Bulgaria, or to Moscow, or to
Beijing. But it takes no convincing at all to get someone
to move to Paris.

Glenda and I decided, okay, let them convince us!

If we were to face the rigors, the stresses, the difficulties,
of life in Paris, with its art and its cafés and its croissants
and its rich, rewarding culture, then we wanted to be sold
on the idea.

We were suitably wined and dined.

They put us in the George V Hotel. They took us to
Regine's. They took us to Maxim's.

Would we like Paris?

To this day, Glenda and I laugh about it.

"Gee," we said, "maybe we could do this!"

So off we went to France in 1972.

Language is crucial for American businesspeople working in foreign countries. You don't have to be fluent, but
you must be able to communicate.

Before I left I took a total-immersion course in French.
It was tough. I had three instructors. They would get tired
and rotate. They would take me to lunch and I could only
speak French, quite an unusual experience, since I was sitting in a restaurant in Detroit.

At least it gave me a running start.

I was going to be Ford's man inside a company that
should never have been bought by Ford in the first place.
The story about the stock, the ancient security guard, the
drill press, the pistol-packing gendarmes, and the wild rush
to J.P. Morgan was just a small slice of this disaster.

Richier S.A. was beyond saving and had been bought by

Ford for all the wrong reasons. Only five people in the company of six thousand were willing to speak English.

But that wasn't the biggest problem.

The biggest problem was that Richier was already dead, but Ford just didn't know it. I should have looked at the situation more closely before hiring on, but I didn't. I should have said, "Hold it, no thanks."

But that wasn't what I was thinking about at the George V and Maxim's and Regine's. All I was thinking about was magnificent Paris.

I didn't realize until later that I was going to be Ford's key man in what amounted to a business Bulgaria, admittedly with very good food.

Richier had been created by the original inventor of the tower crane.

Tower cranes have become familiar in the United States, but at that time, they were only common in Europe, where they were used to construct most buildings.

Richier business kept growing, and by the time Ford arrived, it was operating in two hundred countries. It produced just about any kind of equipment you can think of to make high-rise buildings or roads.

Cement mixers. Road graders. You name it, Richier made it.

The company had always been able to grow with each passing year, so no one ever paid any attention to the costs. As long as the revenue numbers kept climbing, everyone thought everything was okay. (Not a good idea to mistake sales top-line growth for success.)

The moment competition showed up, the place was dead because sales stopped growing but costs kept rising.

Despite the French national proclivity to own their own companies, they simply gave up. They couldn't sell it to anyone in France, so they said yes to Ford.

The folks at Ford who looked at the deal made a big mistake.

They thought, "Well, what a great deal. Look at all the

stuff this company makes, and we can buy it for $165 million!" That was what they had to pay to buy the shares of stock. They didn't look at the fact that there was another $400 million in debt. And they didn't look at the fact that they would have to cover years of continuing losses before the company could be turned around, if ever.

As I said, they were swayed by the revenue numbers without looking at the real costs.

I had nothing to do with buying the place, I am happy to say. But it was a great lesson for me. When you buy the shares of a company you are taking on a major employee responsibility for all their pay, separation, retirement, and medical benefit requirements.

You are taking on the full burden of debt and any ongoing losses.

You had better do all that with your eyes open.

But Ford didn't consider any of that. It didn't look at operating losses. It didn't look at debt. It didn't look at pensions.

I went in as the chief financial officer, but in reality, I was the senior Ford person.

I kept running into situations that amazed me.

I was there for two weeks and met my new treasurer. He was a Belgian from Ford there. He was picked because he was a good treasurer and he was trilingual. He came to see me and said he had had a strange experience.

He said he went to lunch in the company cafeteria. There were no empty tables, so he sat down by a stranger and introduced himself. His new lunchmate told him that he was responsible for investor relations. My treasurer asked this man whom he worked for.

He said he didn't work for anybody.

"How is that possible?" the treasurer asked.

"Well, I have been trying to work for someone in this company for fifteen years, and I can't find anybody who will let me work for them," the man said.

So I told my treasurer, "Go back and tell him he works for you."

The Belgian thought that was unusual. He came from a less direct, more polite world.

But he did what I asked. He came back to me later and told me he was really sorry he had approached the man, because the minute he told him he now had someone to work for, "He was delighted to unburden his problems on me."

They weren't small problems.

Richier was displaying no vital signs.

My assumption had always been that if a company had minus net worth, it had passed away. But in Paris, I learned a magical financial trick. I call it financial levitation. With it, you can keep a company alive for a long time even if it is dead.

We did it for two years.

There were two fellows at Ford who were responsible for buying the company. One of them was very bright, had graduated from Yale at age eighteen, and had a brilliant career at Ford. His only flaw was that he could not utter the sentence "I made a mistake." He would never say to me that Richier was dead, but he did everything he could do to help levitate it with me. I am certain that he realized after two months of experience that there was no hope for this company.

The former owner was producing so many products and selling them in so many places in such small volume that there was just no way to put this Humpty-Dumpty company back together. We needed to simplify it and identify the products that made money and expand on those. But there were so many fixed costs that revenue kept dropping faster than costs as we weeded out low-volume products.

The only answer was to take each product line and sell it to some other company whose primary business was that product. And that is what we did. We levitated for two years until we could sell it in pieces.

Companies can drive themselves into the grave chasing incremental profits. Richier had assumed it could create enough volume and enough price to pay for materials. But 101 products and two hundred countries later, it wasn't working.

One day, the annual revenue growth stops, and with all of those fixed costs, you die. The lesson learned: Contain and control your costs, count all your costs, allocate your costs to every product, and price to make a profit. If you do that, you can have a healthy company that isn't digging itself deeper and deeper into trouble.

I had a great run-in with what I call myths and legends when I worked with communist labor unions at Richier. I knew my union history, of course. But I had had no experience with the leftist unions of Europe. The assumption was that communists were all terrible and that communist unions were all destructive.

Given half a chance, they would wreck a company just so the workers would become doubly angry and become communists, too. This was part of the world conspiracy theory, an assumption that Moscow had tentacles that reached everywhere and was calling all the shots.

Wrong.

These French communists were real pragmatists.

I could do deals with them. I could negotiate with them. I could understand where they were coming from.

They didn't understand business and they did, indeed, view me as a capitalist, and double ugly because I was an American capitalist. But they knew how to deal, as opposed to the other unions inside that company.

Those other fellows would just show up one day and announce they were going on strike. I would ask how we could fix the problem. What could we do to avoid the strike?

And they would say, "Nothing."

Then you would find out that the problem wasn't with Richier at all, but that there was some national complaint afoot and the whole union movement had decided to walk out about it.

Politics was usually at the heart of it.

It was a good carry-away for me.

Don't believe what you hear. Always go out and find out for yourself. The communists were only concerned about protecting jobs for their people.

You had to cut through the polemics and the posturing to understand that, but saving jobs was what it was all about for them.

And yes—you can deal with people like that.

I have the same sense about the Chinese communists. They are nominally communist and they use some of the same phrases.

But at heart, they are extraordinarily pragmatic, and that creates an atmosphere in which a businessperson can deal.

One part of Richier was still all about cranes.

We thought, "Well, if cranes are so important, why not build the biggest crane in the world?"

We wanted to design it for shipbuilding. People who build the hulls of ships work very quickly on the inside, but working on the outside is a different matter. Everything slows down because of the amount of scaffolding that has to be put in place and the awkward positions workers need to be in to weld and rivet.

The Richier idea was that we could design a gigantic crane so that when the workers were done inside the hull, we could put straps around it, lift it, and turn it upside down. That would make the outside work a lot easier.

We made a monster tower crane. It was very tall. The operator sat in a little booth up on top. It seemed as though it would work. But we had not factored in the possibility of the hundred-year wave arriving (the worst-case scenario) in a protected harbor just as we were testing our new product.

What happened was a lot like something you used to see in old Warner Brothers cartoons.

We had a hull in the water with straps around it.

Then the wave came into the harbor and lifted the hull.

That took all of the tension off the crane cables.

Then the wave moved back out to sea and the full weight of the hull pulled down on the crane.

A fail-safe device in the crane motor clicked in, but the pull was so severe and so sudden that the motor of the crane blew up.

Then the crane started to sway. And sway severely. In the cartoon version, the operator would have been flung from the booth and would have landed safely, head first, in a big tub of something gooey.

But this was no cartoon.

The operator was sitting up there in his tiny booth 150 feet above the ground in the swaying tower, undoubtedly having thoughts of death.

It took a while, but the crane finally settled back and stabilized.

The only bad thing that happened to the operator was that he had to climb down, go home, and change his pants.

We decided not to pursue this experiment further.

One of my disappointments at Richier was that I simply could not stop the waterfall of "Do It the Ford Way," whether that made any sense in the French setting or not.

So many big companies make the same mistake. They buy a smaller company—domestic or foreign—and then say, "Here are our rules. Follow them." That undermines creativity and imposes rules or controls or systems that have no application in that smaller company, or in that foreign country.

And it hurts.

This company was already dead.

But Ford seemed determined to kill it a second time with its "Do It the Ford Way" approach.

The work at Richier was extraordinarily frustrating because there was no hope. There was just buying time.

After two years, I told Ford I wanted out of there. I had a fight with one of my Ford bosses. One of the two men who had been the original sponsors inside Ford for the Richier purchase had figured out how to vacate the scene.

But the other one still had Richier around his neck.

He said he needed me, that I was the only Ford person who could understand, who could explain what was going on.

I said, "I have an idea, why don't *you* come in and do it!"

He didn't like that, but in the end, that is what happened. He later was fundamentally responsible for the successful break-up of Richier.

It turned out that he and his family loved Paris, although I am certain he did not like dealing with Richier up close.

That gave me the chance to leave.

My network was developing at Ford. Red Poling, who was chief financial officer of Ford of Europe, later to become CEO of Ford, saw an opening and made my case. Off we went to live in London.

It was 1974 and I was responsible for what Ford called nonautomotive operations, which basically meant everything that wasn't directly connected to making cars.

What an experience!

The global economy has expanded vastly since the 1970s, but the challenge remains the same: getting people to work with one another, even those who may have long, deep, and uncomfortable histories.

The main headquarters was in London, but the operations were all over the U.K., Germany, and Spain, with some functions in all of the European capitals.

I was an electrical power house manager, truck fleet manager, communications manager, security systems manager, housing manager, land acquisition manager, home construction manager, and fleet manager of the ten thousand cars Ford employees used in Europe.

I was surprised to find some remnants from World War II.

Ford was trying to act as though there were one Europe long before there really was one Europe. The company would mix people from England, Germany, Belgium, and the United States. A couple of meeting scenes are enough to describe the war legacies I kept running into.

At lunch one day, one of the Germans was complaining about how difficult it was to find adequate housing and schools in England, at which point one of the British said, "I don't understand why you are complaining. You worked so hard to get here in World War II."

At a session in Brussels, some Belgians, some Germans, and some British were to have a meeting. The German contingent was late. When they arrived, they said, "We are late because one of your Belgian bridges collapsed. Don't you Belgians know how to build bridges?"

And one of the Belgians said, "Well, there was a time that we built bridges to last for a hundred years, but it was such a waste, because every thirty years or so, you would come along and blow them up."

Word came from Detroit that because of a recession, we had to cut costs. The target was a 10 percent cut across the board. Every manager in a big company eventually runs into this kind of edict. Sometimes folks just slash 10 percent and think they have accomplished the task.

That is wrong.

Every division, every component of a business, carries weight, but some areas carry more weight than others; if you look closely, you will find that some areas carry more fat, too.

Why cut 10 percent from an operation that is running efficiently? Why cut only 10 percent from an operation that is full of fat?

After looking at my part of the business, I concluded I could probably take 25 percent of the costs out of my operation. And after twelve months, I did. But you have to know your company well to cut costs that way. Some places you shouldn't even cut 5 percent. But most companies don't take the time, and most bosses aren't ruthless enough to be selective.

It is much easier to just tell everyone to take a 5 or 10

percent cut. But what you end up with is a company that is as much out of balance as before the recession started.

There was a lot of fat in one part of my German operation. I faced an interesting challenge in teaching our Ford Germany people efficiencies in dealing with guest workers.

In the aftermath of World War II, the German government wanted to be very careful to treat non-Germans in an exemplary way. There were thousands upon thousands of guest workers in Germany from Greece, Turkey, Italy, and Yugoslavia.

The government rules required a company to offer them housing, German language training, and bus service. We had high-rise buildings that we leased, enough room for 7,000 guest workers. But we had only 4,500 workers.

When I saw the numbers, I said, "Why do you need these extra buildings if you only have 4,500 guest workers?"

"Well," came the reply, "we are offering these extra spaces to German people." I asked if we were making a profit on it, and I was told that we weren't, but that the spaces were empty anyway so we were offering them at tempting rents.

"Wait a minute," I said. "How about if we stop that?"

My suggestion was that we empty some of the buildings, fill the others, and then get rid of the leases on buildings that were not housing workers. But my German advisers said that wouldn't be wise because we would have to bring all of those buildings back to their original condition. That would increase our costs and the Ford people running Ford Europe wouldn't like that.

So I created a five-year budget. In the first three years, I said, our costs have to be flat. We will spend some money and as we start to close buildings down, we will have enough savings to accelerate the number of buildings we close down. After three years, we will have just enough buildings to house the workers and our costs will drop like a rock.

They didn't believe it, but the plan worked. We saved an enormous amount of money. The only mistake I made, and it was a mistake that taught me a lot of lessons about culture, was to propose putting Greek and Turkish folks in the same guest worker buildings.

There is history there, of course. I would have invented a new form of gunpowder with that decision.

You live, you manage, and you learn.

Henry Ford II was still the big boss when I was in England, and one of my jobs was to build a London meeting facility with bedrooms for overnight stays.

Re-creating a Holiday Inn would not do.

For Henry Ford, that kind of facility had to be perfect. Don't spare the money. These kinds of assignments take many months. They literally reached down to questions about what kind of food the emperor would like and how he would like it prepared. I am sure he would have objected had he known about the fuss, but no one would ever tell him.

We were working with a seventeenth-century building, and we had to jump through hoops with the London city fathers to get the permits to carry out our plan.

By the time we had completed the job, it was perfect.

Well, almost perfect.

Beautiful furnishings, leather furniture that fit the atmosphere. We even collected the perfect wines, all to meet someone's idea of Henry Ford's meticulous standards.

Sometimes, you just can't plan well enough.

On the first night, Ford and the senior officers of the company were settling in at our magnificent newly restored building.

There was only one problem.

We had installed one of those industrial stoves in the kitchen, a fire-breathing monster of a stove that would make any chef proud. We overlooked the fact that a stove that serious needs a lot of insulation.

The workers forgot to insulate the floor. The chefs were

cooking like crazy, and someone noticed the smell of smoke.

Then we all noticed more than the smell of smoke; there was real fire.

We had to evacuate the building and call in the firemen.

I recall thinking, "Well, my career may have ended tonight."

Fortunately, no one ever connected that mistake to me.

I came away from my two years as director of Ford's nonautomotive operations in Europe with some very strong opinions about how big companies should not be managed.

True, I had cut costs by 25 percent, but it was the structure of Ford's European operation that bothered me. The company had created tremendous inefficiencies by layering staffs upon staffs. It had a European staff, and then a staff in each country. It was a huge waste of money and time.

But it certainly changed me.

Ever since, I have been determined to cut the layers out of management. That became fashionable in the 1980s, but I don't think many managers found the right way to do it. Wholesale layoffs and downsizing simply weren't the answer.

The answer is in training the people in line operations well enough from the beginning to do the jobs themselves without a lot of hierarchy and supervision.

It was a valuable education for me, because I was heading again into new territory.

I would still be with Ford, but I would be far from Detroit and very much on my own.

Much to my surprise for a man whose background was in labor and whose experience was in finance and management, I would be building cars.

FOUR

★

Graduate School of Hard Knocks: Running a Business

By 1976, my career at Ford had carried me far beyond the old Edsel division, deeply into the challenges of business around the world and well into the ranks of senior management.

But something was missing. I had watched management at Ford for years, learning from its mistakes and from its brilliance. I knew it was time for me to have something of my own.

I wanted to run my own company.

I got a call from the vice president of Ford of Latin America and he was looking for someone to run the Ford company in Venezuela.

It was an attractive offer. It would be my chance to run a full, although smaller, auto company. In Venezuela, Ford made cars, bought parts from suppliers, sold cars to its own network of dealers, and had its own spare parts depot. It also had its own government and public relations staffs. It was an American auto company in miniature.

I viewed it as my chance to be the big fish in a little pond and learn how to run a complete company. This was February of 1976. The kids were in the middle of their school year.

As compelling as the offer seemed to me, I had been worrying about the impact all my moving around was having on my family.

After two years in London, Glenda and I decided to have

a talk at dinner. I tried to explain to my children what I was doing and why I was doing it, why there had been so many moves. I told them we would try to stay put until the three older ones graduated from high school.

At that point, our teenagers looked at us and said something that seemed surprising to parents who thought it had been hard for them to leave friends and familiar places.

"But all our friends get to move around."

They had made friends everywhere they lived, and they knew moving was part of the contract.

I decided I would go to Venezuela by myself, followed two months later by my oldest son, whom I put in school in Caracas. Glenda and the other three children would stay in London until June, when the school year ended.

That might sound absurd because it involved a lot of complicated commuting for six months. I would work for three weeks in Venezuela, then go to London for a week. But it taught me a good lesson about executives and how they focus on their jobs. The conflict between family and work has always been difficult for me.

But this situation seemed ideal. I would have three weeks of the month full of nothing but work (and keeping my eye on my oldest son) and then one week full of nothing but family. There I was in Caracas, Venezuela, with a new job full of demands, trying to go through a quick learning curve, working on my Spanish.

I could work all of the hours I wanted with a clear conscience for three weeks and then I would jump on a plane and go to London. The phone system in Venezuela was terrible and there was a big time difference, so there was no chance I could continue my work from London by phone. Glenda and I and the three children had plenty of time together for one week a month, although it was a little like getting to know my family anew each month.

I was surprised by what I found in Venezuela.

Ford was not very well managed there, and that was unfortunate because a tremendous opportunity was sitting at its doorstep. We had about a quarter of the market, in a virtual tie with General Motors.

The government of Venezuela was full of itself. The price of oil had quadrupled and Venezuela was an oil-exporting country. It was a heady time, so heady, in fact, that the government had decided it knew a lot more about running companies than anyone else and had passed a complicated series of decrees on how it was to be done.

The effect of this government intervention was that the auto industry in Venezuela had ground to a halt. It took me about six weeks on the job to realize that ultimately all those government decrees were not going to be implemented. They would have permanently killed the fledgling auto industry.

But all of the auto company executives who had been in the country for a while didn't realize that. They were afraid to make investments. They didn't know whether to go forward or backward. They were frozen in place.

I sensed a great opportunity for Ford and for myself and picked up a valuable lesson at the same time.

If all the other businesses are frozen in place, then the first one to move is going to succeed. I seized the opportunity. It was an extraordinary run. Picture a footrace that begins with a man firing a starting gun. I felt as though I was the only person who could hear the *bang* when the starter pulled the trigger.

I started running, and everyone else was standing still.

During three years, the profits of this little Ford company went from $10 million to $100 million a year. Our market share went from 24 percent to 48 percent. Employment tripled from two thousand to six thousand.

How did we do that? The short answer is: big cars.

A few of us talked it out. We didn't want to offend the government, but we were certain that we had ripe opportunities because Venezuela's economy was growing so quickly. It was frontier democracy, though. The money was not evenly spread. But there was a growing wealthy class of people who could well afford a couple of cars.

The bigger the car, the better.

And the price of gas was 23 cents a gallon.

We decided to concentrate on Ford trucks and full-sized cars. We were also able to attract to Ford the best of the Venezuelan auto dealers. We had a plan for them, and for our suppliers.

By picking Ford trucks and big cars, we were focusing on the high-profit end of the market. We didn't want to squeeze the dealers. We wanted to help them have good profit margins so they could reinvest. So we decided we were not going to increase the number of dealers as quickly as we were increasing the volume of trucks and big cars. That meant we would be sending more high-profit vehicles to each of the dealers. That way, we were able to attract the best dealers.

I have always wanted to spend some time counting the number of people I helped make rich over my career. And boy, were there a lot of them in Venezuela. All you needed was a Ford dealer franchise and you could be a millionaire.

I felt like an industrial soldier.

I would establish the beachhead. I could create the assembly plant, then we would wave in the U.S. auto part suppliers and then the U.S. banks. In the process, I was helping to create a local management structure in Venezuela that would be capable later of doing the job itself.

(I think the United States lost that role, that industrial soldier role, to the Japanese beginning in the early 1980s. Even though the Japanese expansion has moderated some, even now it is impressive. The Japanese were able to play that role even in the United States. They found a way to exploit all the classic issues in the auto business. I had a sense that was coming when I was in Venezuela. I knew that American expansion was crucial, but that was an aggressiveness the U.S. was about to lose.)

*   *   *

While I was successful and had a great time in Venezuela, I made one of my career's biggest mistakes there.

I was still this hotshot, full of confidence, forty-one years old and willing to take risks. I was running fast and I was talking fast.

Too fast.

There was a management team working with me and they weren't articulate enough to say, "Jerry, you're pushing us too fast. We don't know what we're doing. We're going to fall on our face."

The management experts came in from Detroit and said maybe we needed manufacturing managers who were fluent in Spanish. So we brought in a team from Mexico. That was worse. We brought in managers from Argentina. That was even worse.

But it wasn't their fault, it was mine. I didn't listen to them.

We got ourselves into manufacturing trouble so deep that we had to cut way back on production and then start it back up again.

It was two years after I had arrived.

I was determined to ramp up production even faster.

The economy was booming and the demand for big cars and trucks was strong. I didn't want to miss my chance. When I showed up, we were producing 150 cars a day. I pushed that to 300 a day. We upped it to four hundred cars a day, and that's when trouble hit.

I knew we had a problem when cars were coming off the end of the assembly line missing parts.

We couldn't ship them to dealers in that condition, so we would put them out in the yard to wait for the missing parts to arrive to complete them. It was an elegant junkyard full of cars missing parts, some without axles, some without trim, some without steering wheels.

The first time that happened to us, I should have known better. But I thought at the time that letting the cars sit in the lot to wait for parts was a good idea. All the signs were there telling me to cut back, but I didn't see them.

There were two problems.

We did not have the manufacturing experience and worker experience to build four hundred cars a day. We needed a slower ramp-up to test new facilities and train people.

Second, we had this pipeline from suppliers, most of them in the U.S., but we had lost control over that part of the business as we increased car production. We were getting the wrong parts in the wrong containers. Some of our parts ended up sitting in a port somewhere, and we had to spend time and money trying to find them.

It took almost a year to solve the problem by bringing production and supply back into line.

Much later in my career, I saw the same problem at Boeing during an experience that seemed a lot like Venezuela déjà vu.

Because I was a customer, and because they were talented, salt-of-the-earth people, I was trying to encourage them.

I said, "Look, if you have been in the manufacturing business long enough, one of these things is going to happen to you. You forget that manufacturing a complex product is not routine. You forget because all of the parts show up magically, every day, for years. And you just think that that is the way life is.

"Then one day, some parts don't show up on time, at which point you are back to the beginning of the Industrial Revolution. You don't know with confidence when you are going to get back on track. You have got to slow things down and start rebuilding."

I was able to pass that advice along because I had been there myself. These kinds of problems happen because you turn your back on the manufacturing process and ignore the day-to-day routine instead of checking on it all the time. And it can get really bad if you ramp up too quickly or try to introduce new products too fast.

*   *   *

After a couple of years, I realized the Venezuelans never had a chance to get their roots as a society. They jumped right out of being an agrarian society to being an oil-producing society. Somewhere between 1910 and 1915, some wildcat oil folks, Dutch and Texans, showed up. Crude, tough whiskey drinkers, they helped create the culture I found in Venezuela.

Venezuelans never really had the work ethic embedded. They could work for extraordinary money in the oil fields. Later, the government nationalized the oil companies and then siphoned off the revenues. In good times, they had an idyllic welfare state. Their attitudes toward work were different from ours and unfamiliar to most Americans.

How does an American-trained executive tap that kind of workforce to build cars?

We paid our folks above the local standard. I was lucky because Ford's assembly plants and parts depots were located in a place where there wasn't a temptation to run off to work in the oil fields. I think we had some very good workers. We were the best job in the area. But we still had to wrestle with Venezuelan work habits.

Even though we paid well, it was still hard to convince people to work overtime. We tried to build some sense of belonging by holding lots of employee parties.

Almost everywhere, beer helps in building employee loyalty.

But I learned during that experience that some of our workers in Venezuela had an unusual sense of marital fidelity.

We held our first party.

The fellow who ran it said we spent a lot more money than we thought we would spend because we misjudged the number of girlfriends the men would bring to the event. Some would bring their girlfriends, and their wives. He was very apologetic. He said that in the future, we would limit attendance to one wife and one girlfriend.

*   *   *

American businesspeople develop their own communities wherever they live. Your first task seems to be making those connections, looking for familiar people you can be comfortable with. I called on my neighbors within a few days of arrival to introduce myself. As it turned out, they had a son the same age as my oldest son.

Within thirty days, my executive neighbor, Bill Niehaus, was kidnapped.

Immediately, the U.S. embassy and the Venezuelan Secret Police talked to me. It was very disconcerting. One of the policemen said he was surprised that I had not been the target, because Ford was the biggest foreign-owned company in Venezuela and I was a more likely candidate for kidnapping.

My neighbor's kidnapping was the first in years, and there weren't any after it. Some men—real pros at kidnapping—dressed in army uniforms showed up at his door. The cleaning lady answered. Within ninety seconds, the five people in the house were tranquilized. Bill was taped up and hauled off.

The Venezuelan Secret Police said they wanted to give me a bodyguard. I thought about this for a while, and eventually agreed. It is impossible to stay on guard yourself. You cannot spend all your time thinking about your own safety. Pretty soon, your mind drifts to other things.

My bodyguard and I were the odd couple. I was the businessman. He weighed 225 pounds, all muscle, and carried a big revolver. It didn't take long before I started to worry about him. Did he have breakfast? Did he have a day off? How was he doing? What do you do with a guy like this? Do you bring him along to business meetings? Do you park him outside?

Do you throw him a sandwich?

He would call his Secret Police office three times a day to see whether anything was up. Sometimes, he would forget and leave his gun sitting on the telephone stand. My

younger children would soon be coming to Venezuela. I
didn't need pistols lying around. After about six weeks, I
decided I just couldn't do it anymore. I got some training
in precautions and defensive measures. Don't follow the
same route every day. I didn't reveal my schedule.

We had an electronic alarm system installed at home
and in the office.

Fortunately, I never needed the police. The alarm at
home went off by accident one day and it took the police a
day and a half just to find my house. As a silly form of status, the houses in our area of Caracas didn't have addresses.
They had names. Even if you were a cop, you had to have at
least a few dry runs before you could find anyone.

By the way, Bill Niehaus's kidnapping lasted for three
and a half years. After three months, the experts thought
he was probably dead.

Bill was not dead. But he was on the move all of the time.
Three and a half years after his kidnapping, he was being
held in the jungle near a small town. The local police were
chasing some cattle thieves. The kidnappers heard them
and scattered.

The police found Bill. He looked like Howard Hughes
by this time, thin, very long hair, long fingernails. He told
the local police who he was and they got scared, thinking
those professional terrorists would come back and kill
them. So they ran away.

There sits Bill, all alone in the camp. He gets up and
walks to the nearest road. He follows the road to a farm,
where he makes a call to his company in Ohio. They send
a jet, and he ends up in Ohio.

I was too busy in Venezuela, and perhaps a bit too young,
to be scared by the possibility of kidnapping.

My concerns were about production.

We wanted to find a way to produce even more luxury
cars and bigger trucks. But I couldn't figure out how to get
around one of the Venezuelan government's toughest

rules. Even though it was a small country, they wanted cars produced in Venezuela, but they didn't want to let auto manufacturers produce too many different cars.

I stumbled onto an idea.

I was talking to a German-Venezuelan family, the Zinggs.

They had the franchise to produce Mercedes products in Venezuela. The government was demanding that the Zinggs start increasing the local content of their cars. They either had to buy more car parts in Venezuela or make more of the car there and not import.

The Zingg family factory was in another, even more remote part of Venezuela. It was a small factory with limited production. Mercedes had restricted them to importing full kits. They are called knockdown cars. All they had to do was bolt them together and paint.

Daimler-Benz was very reluctant to gamble the quality of their cars just to let Venezuelans make more parts to meet government local content requirements. The relationship was starting to crack between Daimler-Benz and the Zingg family because of this government pressure.

Even if they wanted to, the Zinggs couldn't sell their rights to produce Mercedes cars and trucks, although that is what I wanted.

I would have used that factory to build Lincoln Continentals and Ford heavy trucks.

But that wasn't going to happen.

So I came up with a scheme.

I decided to rent their whole company by guaranteeing them a fixed annual profit.

It would take some persuading, because the Zingg family was risk-averse. I thought a visit from Henry Ford II was in order. He had his faults, but he could be great company and was a terrific salesman for the Ford Company. I wanted him to come to Venezuela to meet this family and reassure them.

I explained my plan. I wanted to bring in some people from one of our other plants, transfer some local Venezuelan managers, add some Americans, and start building luxury cars and big trucks. The Ford people in the U.S. thought I was nuts. They often thought I was nuts, but each time I succeeded at a novel idea, they were less willing to stop me.

The Zinggs were flattered that Henry Ford was coming to visit. They brought out some of their boats. They didn't just have one boat, they had several boats. For Henry Ford, there was a ninety-five-foot boat and a sixty-five-foot boat. Off we went to visit an archipelago off Venezuela, one of the most beautiful places I have ever seen.

The Zinggs had made a deal. The archipelago was treated as a national treasure by the Venezuelan government, so only the fishermen who lived there could build on the land. Many of the islands inside the reef that formed this enormous saltwater lake were white sand and too low to have fresh water.

The Zinggs got one of the fishermen to agree that they would bring him water and medicine and other supplies he might need from time to time if he would build a little "guest house" to their specifications.

On the appointed day, we arrived.

I was with Henry Ford and the Zinggs. We were greeted by this friendly-looking, grizzled fisherman missing half his teeth. He was probably fifty years old, but because he had spent his life in the sun, he looked about eighty. He had not shaved. His clothing was unkempt.

He immediately threw his arms around Henry Ford and the senior Zingg and all three of them became instant pals.

It remains one of my fondest business memories.

They were sitting in the hut, drinking beer and laughing. This fisherman had no idea who Henry Ford was and cared even less. They were just having a good time in his thatched hut, sitting on some folding chairs.

It was a great visit. The project worked well.

I didn't know it at the time, but another Ford acquaintance had plans for me.

These plans would change my life, and my address again, in a big way.

FIVE

⭑

Am I Nuts? Taking the World's Toughest Job

Venezuela. Christmas of 1978.

Glenda and I had just come home from a party and there was a message waiting for me.

"Call Iacocca."

I looked at the message. Lee had gone to Chrysler only two months earlier. I assumed he wanted to know something about Chrysler operations in Latin America. Glenda looked at the message and without saying anything else, she said, "Don't call back."

She had great intuition and did not want to move.

But I did call back.

Iacocca said he wanted to talk to me about coming to Chrysler to take the controller's role. I went to see him a couple of times in different cities in the U.S. I was traveling incognito, because the last thing I wanted was for Ford to find out I was talking to Iacocca. There was anger when he left Ford and he was now determined to salvage one of Ford's key competitors.

I told Iacocca I didn't want to come to Chrysler as controller because I was already running my own company for Ford in Venezuela.

I decided to talk to my friends.

Every time I told them what my choices were, they told me not to be stupid, that Chrysler was in deep trouble. I got up to about my ninth telephone call and everybody I was talking to said I was crazy. I had a great career going so I should just forget about Chrysler.

I had my own thoughts. I knew I was a home run hitter in the minor leagues. I had carried Ford of Venezuela from $10 million to $100 million in profits in a very short period. But getting the call from Iacocca was like being asked suddenly if I wanted to play in the World Series.

I couldn't get that out of my head.

Glenda wanted to know why I was calling all those people. I told her I was trying to get some advice. She said, "You are not. You are going to keep calling until one person agrees with you. You might as well save the phone bills. Let's go."

So we did.

I thought I had better get to Detroit and tell my Ford bosses what I was doing. I didn't want to give Iacocca a final yes until I had talked to the Ford people. I talked to my boss. I talked to his boss. They all presented a simple case: "Are you nuts? You have a good career going here."

But I couldn't get them to tell me what they meant by having "a good career going here." I wanted more certainty that I was on my way up at Ford. What would my next job be?

Once I had made my decision, it was amazing how quickly my Ford bosses turned on me. They would have nothing to do with me. They just turned me over to the personnel people. If I could negotiate a good departure, fine. And if I couldn't, tough luck. The personnel people sensed it, too, and they were not on their best behavior. It was very unpleasant.

It must feel like spouses coming apart and heading for divorce. I thought about when a husband and wife conclude that it is over and the lawyers take over and the anger begins. That is how I felt. My company family disowned me in twenty-two minutes after twenty-two years.

It made me a little angry.

I concluded, "The hell with this. I am on my way."

But first, I wanted to say goodbye to Henry Ford II.

It was a Wednesday morning. I showed up at his inner sanctum. I waited about fifteen minutes, then he opened the door and said, "Come in, I am with my brother." William Clay Ford had never operated deep in the company, but he was a major owner. He stayed.

Henry Ford looked at me and said, "This is the dumbest thing I have ever heard. Why would you do this?"

I kept struggling to explain. I didn't even know why I had this great need to have Henry Ford II understand. I wanted him to understand, but he kept talking.

"Why would you go with that Iacocca?"

Finally, it clicked.

I said, "Mr. Ford, do you remember your own feelings when you were twenty-seven years old just after World War II and Ford was in trouble and you came to this company to run it? Do you remember the excitement, the challenge?"

He said, "Yeah."

"Chrysler is a mess, I suppose, but that is why I want to do it," I told him.

He paused and looked at me.

Then he reached his hand across the desk and he said, "I want to wish you great success."

He was very nice to me from that point forward, even up to his death.

There was a lesson in that farewell.

If I had not taken the time to say goodbye to Henry Ford, my departure from the company would have been defined by all those people who thought I was literally nuts for going to Chrysler.

I got to deliver my message myself. I could say it my way, clearly and directly.

I landed in Detroit from Caracas, right in the middle of a family crisis.

My daughter had been thrown out of her boarding school,

which was in a Detroit suburb. She had committed a minor offense. She and her friends had written some messages on a kitchen wall in peanut butter.

What a surprise, seventeen-year-olds writing on the wall with peanut butter! That was it. But it happened as the staff of the school had decided it was time to tighten up on mis-behavior. She was out. She could go to class, but she couldn't board there.

She had nowhere to go. Her family was in Venezuela and her father was jumping into a job almost everyone thought he was nuts for taking.

Well, I told her, I'll get a temporary two-bedroom apart-ment in Detroit. Come on in and we will figure it out. In-advertently, she became my press secretary. It was Detroit, and my arrival was a big deal. Chrysler was a big story, and I was the latest development, Iacocca's biggest steal.

I was getting a lot of press calls I just wasn't ready to han-dle. She was my intermediary buffer. When I returned for a week to pack up in Venezuela, she ended up living for a while with the Iacoccas, a gesture that bonded me to that family.

Finding safe harbor for my daughter wasn't the only problem.

I have never been the kind of fellow to buy as much clothing as I could afford. I packed up 75 percent of my clothing in two great big suitcases in Venezuela. I remem-ber putting them on the curb while I was transferring to a flight to Detroit at La Guardia in New York. They gave me the baggage claim tickets.

I never saw my clothing again.

There I was, showing up at Chrysler, a company in chaos, and I didn't have any clothing. And I didn't have any time to buy clothing. I wore the same suit, shirt, and tie, for five days.

If it were a movie about Chrysler, the collapsing car com-pany, my role would have been the disheveled financial ex-ecutive. I was perfectly dressed for it.

A Major Motion Picture: *Chrysler Crumbles. Costumes by Edith Head. Featuring: Lee Iacocca and Me!*

I was ending twenty-two years with a company that had given me a wonderful experience. I had lived on three continents and learned three languages. Could I have become the CEO of a major company sooner?

Maybe.

But I wouldn't give up those experiences for any CEO's title.

I am always reminded about one of those questions about life.

An old man faces the eternal query: "What would you have done differently?"

He answers, "I would have taken more risks."

I had already taken plenty.

But I was about to take the biggest business risk of my life.

The day I walked in, Chrysler was a disaster.

It took me a while to fully understand that, though.

Sometimes, an executive gets so energized and excited by the challenge he faces that it affects his vision. That is a kind way of saying I had not looked closely enough at Chrysler. I didn't take the time to do enough due diligence. I had ended twenty-two years at Ford at the top of my game.

It took a while to get through some really scary times.

I joined Chrysler as vice president and controller. I didn't want to do that because I had just run what amounted to my own company, Ford of Venezuela. But Lee Iacocca had a compelling argument.

He said he knew I liked running things, but he needed me to serve as controller for two years. Then, he said, he would create a truck division and it would be mine to run.

That was my carrot. I was only two years away from running my own, even bigger business again.

That is not the way it played out.

Instead of running that mythical carrot on a stick, the truck division, I ran the effort to save the company.

It was a big job.

I had to convince the federal government to back loan guarantees, to convince the unions to agree to concessions, to convince Chrysler's suppliers to give us some time and money to solve our problems, and to convince four hundred banks all over the world to cut us some slack and sign on to the plan we worked out.

Even now, so many years later, it feels like a job that took up every minute of my waking life for years, an amalgam of exhilaration and exhaustion. I had been in situations before where there was no time, and I had been in situations before where there was no money.

At Chrysler in 1979, I faced both.

My initial impression of Chrysler was that it was a company run by financial engineers. They knew how to manipulate balance sheets and financial statements. But they didn't know how to motivate people or run the day-to-day operations or sort out the operations strategy of the business.

I didn't know how serious the problem was until I got a good look at the numbers. I calculated that if we sold every car we had on hand, we would still face a huge first-quarter loss in 1979. As it turned out, we set an ugly record, a loss of $250 million, the biggest quarterly loss in American business history. Most of the cars did not move in that quarter.

How did Chrysler get into such trouble?

One classic example of the problem was Chrysler's sales bank.

A lot of modern companies have versions of the sales bank. One of the best recent examples was at Sunbeam. Here is how it works.

To make the financial statement look better, you force-feed a tremendous amount of your product into your distributors and dealers. Even if you don't get paid for the shipments, you can lend them the money to pay you. On the financial records, it looks as if you had made a sale.

But sooner or later, you have to 'fess up, because all of that inventory is in the distributors' hands and distributors can't sell it fast enough, so they are not ordering anything new. Everything backs up.

In the case of the sales bank at Chrysler, other car manufacturers had long since learned that the only right way to sell cars was not to produce them unless you had a specific order for that particular car from a dealer.

Whole systems have evolved to handle this part of the car business. Three months in advance you get a bulk order from the dealers. By the time you are actually assembling that car, you have an order for the specific vehicle, its color and its options. When the car comes to the end of the assembly line, the dealer pays for it.

But that is not how it worked at Chrysler.

Chrysler built its cars on speculation. The company would forecast what car buyers and dealers would want (which Chrysler always did poorly), which colors, which options, which models. Then Chrysler would build the cars hoping that their sales would match up with dealer orders before the cars moved off the end of the production line.

But the dealers were smart.

"I'm not sure I want them," was the typical dealer comment.

But Chrysler built the cars anyway, and then put them in a huge lot to wait until dealers wanted them. Dealers had not committed, so basically it was cars sitting in parking lot limbo, waiting for demand to develop.

The dealers loved this.

After about a month, management at Chrysler would say, "Whoops" (or something stronger), and then conclude it would be best to offer discounts to the dealers to move the cars. Then Chrysler folks would work their way down through the sales bank, gradually selling and clearing all those cars off the parking lots.

In good times, that would happen fairly quickly. In bad times, the mismatched cars with the wrong colors and the wrong options would sit there for months.

Chrysler had paid workers and suppliers to build the cars, but the cash was not coming in from dealers. Debt was climbing in the meantime. But all of this was masked because the accountants just booked the cars as valuable Chrysler inventory.

In turn, the dealers generally had the wrong choice of cars to sell and they would also have to discount prices to move them to customers. It made the dealers temporarily happy, though, because they were able to buy cars at very low prices, lower than any other dealer organization in America.

It made things look better for Chrysler, because the cars immediately shifted into "inventory." The expense involved in producing them became part of "inventory" instead of being charged against the expenses of the company.

The second problem was that because these Chrysler folks were financial engineers, they paid little attention to the operating side. They would let the operating people bloat up the number of employees beyond need. You would think the financial people would say, "Forget it, you shouldn't hire anybody." But that's not what happened. They let the operating people make those decisions.

Behind the scenes, one of those bad old formulas of American management was at work. Managers were judged and paid in part on how big their organization was. So if I were a manager and I had a hundred people working for me, I was going to get a higher rating and more pay than someone with, say, fifty people. Give smart people dumb incentives, and they will do dumb things.

When the operating people faced the financial folks, they were able to get by with that old, traditional line of bull: "Why do you think I could do this job with fewer than two hundred people?" Because of that, the company's numbers were severely bloated and the bosses did not understand the business enough to push back.

The other problem was that the financial engineers at Chrysler were just too late in recognizing that the car business was a worldwide business. Ford had been a multinational company since 1914, when it started production in Argentina. General Motors later moved into world markets, too.

Chrysler was very late getting into that game, and it got into it in the wrong way.

An operating person might say, "Well, we are late, but we better take our time and build slowly." But these folks said, "Nope, we are going to run around the world and buy up other companies." And what they bought was garbage. They bought a company in France called Simca, one in Spain called Barrieros, another in England called Rootes.

Even with very good automotive operating people, these companies would have had a difficult time bouncing back. But in the case of Chrysler, they didn't have enough good operating people, and worse, they didn't have operating people with any international experience.

By the time I showed up, those international companies had been dragging Chrysler down rather than helping it.

I was struggling with my learning curve at Chrysler and trying to find out about the auto business in America. I had not followed the American auto business very closely during the three years I was running Ford in Venezuela.

In retrospect, I wish that I had, because then I would have been more comfortable in my TV confrontation with Ralph Nader.

I didn't need a new media lesson, but Chrysler was becoming a big story, and because of that, public relations was taking on a bigger role.

The head of public relations came to see me and said Iacocca had been invited to be on television with Ted Koppel on a show called *Nightline*.

Could I do it?

"Sure, I'll try. What's *Nightline*?"

The plan was for me to appear on *Nightline* with Koppel and Senator William Proxmire of Wisconsin. We were going to debate the merits of help from Washington for Chrysler. I had met Proxmire during my Washington visits, and I thought, "Well, sure, I can do this."

So, I showed up at the studios in New York.

The plan changed twenty minutes before airtime.

First, they said, this is not going to be a panel discussion. I would be in New York all by myself, looking at an opaque screen and listening to the conversation through an uncomfortable earplug. Ted Koppel would be in Washington.

Oh, and by the way, they said, Senator Proxmire can't make it.

Ralph Nader is going to take his place.

I looked at our PR guy and I said, "Look, I have been in Venezuela. I can tell you everything about the safety of cars in Venezuela. I can tell you what I used to know about the safety of cars in the United States. What should I do?"

He said he thought we should just take our chances. I would have to go on, he said, because if I didn't, they would never bother to tell anyone they made a switch at the last minute. They would just say that the Chrysler person refused to show up.

So there I sat with this plug, kind of dangling in my ear, staring into an opaque screen, very uncomfortable, and off we went. I had never done that before.

Nader immediately came after me with a question about how we were going to be able to meet all the current safety standards with our new K-car, because it was small and lighter in weight than other cars. I said we were going through all the tests and meeting all the standards and we would only introduce the car once we had met the standards, and not a day before.

Then he wanted to know who was doing the testing.

I said we were testing according to government standards.

And he wanted to know who was doing the testing.

And I said we were meeting the standards.

Then Koppel says, "Will you answer the question?"

I never answered the question because I didn't know the damned answer! The best I can tell you about my *Nightline* experience is that we didn't lose any sales, but we didn't gain any either.

I looked scared, frightened, and out of my element.

Nader was hostile because that was his role.

Koppel was trying to help me, but I was hopeless.

There is an obvious lesson in this experience.

Don't get sucked in. Don't always do what the specialist tells you if it doesn't make sense.

I think our PR person made the wrong call. When all is said and done, you can take advice, but an executive is still responsible for his own decisions. If I had screwed up, I would have hurt Chrysler and wrecked my career.

Chrysler knew it would have to turn to Washington for help. It constructed an intellectually sound argument that never had a chance in hell of getting past the federal government.

Here is how it went.

Washington was passing all sorts of auto laws that affected the production of U.S. automobiles. There were new safety laws. New pollution laws. New fuel economy laws. The auto Big Three were moving to comply with these new standards. But all of this required more people and more investments.

Chrysler argued in Washington that as the smallest of the three auto companies, it faced an unfair situation. Chrysler would have to spend just as much as Ford and General Motors to comply with government regulations, which would make our cost per car higher than for the other two larger companies.

Washington should pay for the difference with some tax credits!

After all, these regulations were in the public interest.

I sat through some meetings listening to this philosophy play out and something didn't ring clear for me. At that time, Iacocca didn't want to have anything to do with Washington. As president, he wanted to get the operations side moving. He wanted to spend 95 percent of his time in Detroit.

That meant John Ricardo, the Chrysler chairman, was spending most of his time in Washington, and he dragged me along occasionally to show some numbers. But the Washington people weren't nodding their heads in response to our argument.

Their reluctance was easy to understand.

If Washington said yes to Chrysler's proposal, then it would have to say yes to the demand for tax credits to the third largest company in every industry.

That wasn't going to happen.

Adding to the problem, Washington would have to admit that there was a real cost penalty for all of these regulations, no free lunch for the consumer or the voter.

The Chrysler plan wasn't worth anything. In the interim, we were bleeding money.

We had a payroll of 140,000 people just for Chrysler. But if Chrysler went under, we were going to drag down about half a million jobs. Suppliers would be out of business. Dealers would be out of business. At the same time, we were watching our sales figures plummet. America was heading into a recession. We dropped from two million cars a year to one million when we bottomed out.

We had to get Chrysler back onto a stronger financial footing. We did that by coming up with a break-even strategy.

We said we would sell all the cars that we could, but that we should be very conservative in financial planning. We assumed we would sell only a million cars a year until we got our new products going.

It was an ugly picture, and I was standing right in the middle of it.

But Iacocca was grabbing hold. He intuitively sensed the urgency of the moment. Chrysler was going to have to change, and it was going to have to change fast.

The company had thirty officers, and it adhered to a genteel tradition at the monthly officer council meetings. There was a big round table, and each officer sat at the table in the order of his seniority with Chrysler. The newest would sit next to the chairman. Because I was hired as controller and vice president, and immediately got dragged into other assignments, particularly in Washington, I didn't show up at my first officer council meeting until the third or fourth month.

Though I was virtually brand-new at the company, I was already sitting at the middle of the table!

Iacocca had washed through half of the officers in the company and replaced them in that three or four months.

We had to switch our Washington tactics. "We're smaller, help us" wasn't selling with the U.S. government.

But there was no way we could turn that company around on our own. We couldn't borrow. The banks would not lend us any more money. And we were bleeding cash.

We gave up quickly on the notion that we could justify tax credits. Instead, we asked for federal loan guarantees.

We did our homework.

To our shock, we discovered that, off the federal balance sheet, there was already about $400 billion in obligations on the part of the federal government that most people didn't know about. They were stealth obligations.

They were mostly guarantees.

It wasn't real money, and if whoever got the loan guarantee performed, the federal government would never have to spend a dime. But if that entity failed, the government would have to write a check to cover the debt.

We decided to ask for $1.5 billion in federal loan guarantees.

We were working with President Jimmy Carter's White House staff. But we would also have to win the support of both houses of Congress, so our primary lobbying time was spent in Washington trying to build support in Congress.

By this time, Chrysler's former chairman was disappearing from the scene.

I became Mr. Washington for Chrysler.

My objective was to plan, orchestrate, and negotiate the loan guarantees in the nation's capital. It was an amazing eye-opener, a high-power lesson in how everything really works.

I got a great lesson early on from the late Tip O'Neill.

He was the Speaker of the House, a Massachusetts veteran who knew exactly how and why everything in Washington worked.

He set me straight.

The big old Democrat put his arm around me one day and said, "Sonny, just being right in this town doesn't cut it."

We were making an extraordinary request.

We were asking for loan guarantees not for an industry, but for a company. There were only a few single entities that had ever received help like that. New York City was one of them, and Lockheed was the other.

I soon found out we had our enemies.

There was a congressman from Florida sitting on a subcommittee and Iacocca was the witness. This congressman sat quietly through much of the hearing until the television cameras went on. Then he jumped up and told Iacocca he was nothing but a con man trying to bilk the taxpayers for money. Then the camera shifted and he sat down again.

I got really interested in this guy.

I found out he had won an election with the campaign

message that he was the only candidate who had officially been declared sane. He had recently come out of an institution.

Later, I learned there really is cosmic justice.

This character so critical of Iacocca later got caught in ABSCAM, the federal sting operation aimed at nailing corrupt congressmen. He was one of the few people who actually went to prison.

The federal agents had a videotape of him cramming what he thought was Arab bribe money into his pockets.

I thought it was so wonderful that he was the one who jumped up and accused Iacocca of being a con man.

On the other side of the experience, there was Jim Blanchard, an eager young congressman from Michigan.

We needed a sponsor for our loan guarantees in the House. But in the early stages, even the Democrats wouldn't touch us because a lot of them were afraid of being burned politically by this strange request from Chrysler.

For some, it was a problem of philosophy.

They thought the federal government should not be meddling in the affairs of companies.

Blanchard had the courage to grab hold, and on the basis of that success, later became governor of Michigan.

I learned early on that there are genuine differences between the Republican and Democratic parties. The assumption has been that they overlap, and they do in many areas. But there are some issues that really separate them.

Even though it sounded like a business-friendly idea, the Republicans viewed the loan guarantee request as a form of industrial policy, which they despised. Remember the tenor of the times: The GOP thought that anything that came from Washington, from education dictates to money for social programs, was bad.

The Democrats were more inclined to help because they viewed the potential collapse of Chrysler, particularly in the midst of a recession, as a drain down which 500,000 jobs would flow.

I also ran into some strong views in the banking community.

The chairman of Citibank, Walter Wriston, said, "Let them die."

He argued that our system required weak companies to disappear (unless they were banks, of course).

John McGillicuddy, head of Manufacturers Hanover, had a more open mind and wanted to see whether the loan guarantees made practical sense or not.

He wanted to wait and accumulate information and then help make the decision. But waiting was dangerous to Chrysler.

We were that close to collapse.

Then there was Senator Russell Long, Democrat from Louisiana.

He was Huey Long's nephew, and he was chock-full of great stories.

"My uncle Huey, he really felt strongly, he really believed in integrity," he told me. "I remember him telling me one day, 'If your political opponent says some really bad things about you, you get out there on that stump and you fight for your integrity. I don't care whether you have to lie, cheat, or steal, you fight for your integrity.'"

Russell Long had an idea, supported by some of the out-of-the-box economic thinkers of the time.

He thought that employee ownership was a good idea and he had passed in Congress legislation called the Employee Stock Ownership Plan (ESOP). I didn't know a darned thing about it at the time, but I would learn plenty about it later at United Airlines.

He called me into his office. He was the Senate Finance Committee chairman at the time.

He said, "You know, most of us southerners are kinda genteel, and we kinda move around issues softly. But I would rather come straight at this. You are going to have an ESOP at Chrysler or you are not going to get a loan guarantee."

I thought, "I need cash. I don't care about employee ownership, I just need to keep this company afloat, so if he needs some employee ownership, he'll get it."

I was thinking at the time that the employees couldn't care less about whether they owned some stock in the company because if we didn't get some cash, the stock would be used for wallpaper and the company would be gone.

But if that was Russell Long's price, then I would pay it.

(It didn't work out very well. We never really had time to educate our employees about stock. So we got into this awful situation later when the employees wanted to sell their stock right away. Doug Fraser, the UAW president, knew the value of the stock and wanted to avoid giving employees the right to sell too quickly. Iacocca and I were thinking the company was bouncing back, but we looked at each other and concluded that you have to stop being your brother's keeper at some point. So we gave the workers a contract giving them the right to sell their stock, and 95 percent of them sold the next day at $16 a share. Before it was over, the stock hit $100. The lesson was obvious: If you want to present a new plan with radical new concepts that involves a large group of people, you have to build in a couple of years of education so people understand what they are doing. This responsibility should not be taken lightly in an America that is shifting away from traditional pension programs and placing more of the responsibility of investing for retirement on employees. In a way, corporate America is asking the individual worker to become a chief financial and pension officer, and some education should go along with that shift in responsibility.)

There was another great character in the middle of the battle to save Chrysler in Washington.

Senator Tom Eagleton of Missouri had been through tough times. He was briefly George McGovern's vice presidential running mate in 1972 but had left the Democratic ticket when it was disclosed he had been treated for mental health problems.

But by 1980 he was a veteran senator and highly respected by everyone in the chamber. Some said that was because he was so smart and experienced, and some added it was also because he was no threat to the other ninety-nine senators who at some point might want to run for president.

Pushing those loan guarantees through Congress gave me a practical lesson in American democracy and how it actually works.

Our forefathers created two houses: the House of Representatives based on population, and the Senate, with two senators from each state.

That structure gave us a strong hint about how to get the loan guarantee legislation through the House.

It took a lot of work. We created computer printouts that showed each House member how many people in their district would lose a job if Chrysler failed.

Then we got some fellows from the unions and some dealers to lobby their congressmen.

Tip O'Neill was right.

Being correct didn't count for much in Washington. But being able to show each member of Congress the value of Chrysler's survival in his or her district made the difference. They wouldn't be voting to save a big company anymore, they would be voting to save individual jobs in their congressional districts.

The people who worked for and were dependent on Chrysler were a clear constituency to which the House responded.

We won our case there.

But we had a terrible time in the Senate.

We had the job-saving argument on our side in a lot of states, but not everywhere. Our proposal in the Senate opened up a whole new level of debate on what it would mean to save Chrysler.

Every state has equal weight in the Senate. It wasn't hard to convince the senators from Michigan and the other industrial states that Chrysler was valuable.

But we had some senators from some of the western states asking, "Tell me one more time. You want me to help you get guarantees from the federal government so you can protect $20 an hour jobs when my constituents in Wyoming get paid $7 an hour? Why should I do that?"

We were at the eleventh hour.

Chrysler was on the line.

Vice President Walter Mondale, the president of the Senate, had special rooms off the Senate chamber. He let us borrow one of them and it became our war room for the Senate vote.

Tom Eagleton sat with us and tried to guide us through what was happening in the Senate. Never known for tidy dress, his shirttail hanging out, he came to us and said he could get six or eight key senators from both sides of the aisle to hold a caucus.

Eagleton told us he would come back and tell us exactly what we could or could not do, but that the time for negotiation was over.

"You'll just have to believe we did the best we could. You will just have to accept it," Eagleton said.

"Well, yeah," was my response.

But there was trouble.

We were to get $1.5 billion in loan guarantees, but we could only use them when we had confirmed we had a business plan to bring Chrysler back to life. We had to get that plan approved by a loan guarantee board.

I had already met some of the requirements, but I believed it would take a few months for us to fulfill the rest.

But we didn't have the money to run Chrysler for a few months.

I wanted some interim guarantees. But even in the Carter administration, there was resistance. The Treasury Department opponents thought if we got the interim money, we would never develop a plan to take the bitter medicine we needed to turn Chrysler around.

Eagleton returned from his caucus after three hours.

"Here is what you can have and what you cannot have," he said.

"You cannot have any interim funds."

I knew we had enough cash left for about two weeks and that we weren't going to make it. (Ultimately, our suppliers saved us.) But it was crystal clear that Eagleton knew what he was talking about. Chrysler would have no chance without the loan guarantees.

But I thought I had little chance of survival without interim funding.

I said yes to Eagleton and we got the loan guarantees through the Senate. We overcame threats of filibusters from some western senators and some of the Republicans.

I was scared. I didn't get enough sleep. At the same time, the process was magnificent. It was beautiful. It was full of inefficiency, but full of glorious democracy, too.

We worked to get those guarantees through Congress from July of 1979 until just before Christmas. Fifteen hours a day, almost every day. The guarantees were signed into law by President Carter on January 7, 1980.

Then two bad things happened.

On January 20, 1981, Ronald Reagan became president. That, in itself, wasn't bad. But his new secretary of the treasury, Don Regan, thought loan guarantees were just nuts. As it turns out, Regan did not get along with Iacocca. If the Republican Treasury Department could have, they would have undone the loan guarantee package.

Then there was David Stockman, in the powerful position of Reagan's budget director, who had been a young congressman from Michigan and who was more conservative than most Republicans in terms of fiscal issues. He was the only Michigan congressman who had voted against loan guarantees.

Everything became even more difficult.

First we were obliged to submit an operating plan for turning around Chrysler. The guarantee board told us we had to get price reductions from our suppliers, pay cuts from employees, loans from five states, and more loans from Canada to prove that we had a plan to turn the company around.

We also had to have a new product plan with new cars coming. Our banks all had to agree to keep our loans in place for a longer period of time.

I was too dumb to be scared.

But we created an attitude at Chrysler. We didn't know what was going to happen, but we knew we were going to have one or two crises that could destroy the company every day.

We didn't know how we were going to do it, but when these crises arrived, we were going to fix them.

We did little more than work for two and a half years. I never got sick. I never even caught a cold until the day I knew Chrysler was saved and turned around. Just when it was starting to turn around, I got sick for six months.

One thing hit me after another, flu, a headache, a backache. Something was going on in my body that prevented all those ailments from happening when we were saving Chrysler.

If I knew how to re-create it, I would have done it six more times in my life. Executives always dream of having a company in which everyone is focused on the same objective. There was no question at Chrysler. The objective was survival.

We were like star athletes who only run a 100 yard dash and don't care about, think about, or deal with anything else.

We had to get four hundred banks scattered all over the world to sign the same new loan agreement. We tried everything.

We had to deal with banks in Beirut and Tehran. We

begged and we threatened and we cajoled. The deal was all or nothing.

It was tough. All of the banks had to sign, or those that had already signed could renege on the deal.

In the spring of 1980, we were down to the last bank. It was in Rockford, Illinois.

In its bad days, Chrysler reached out further and further to borrow money and would borrow ever smaller amounts from ever smaller banks because that is all it could get.

The bank president in Rockford had it in his mind that nobody was going to tell him to do anything that was not in the interest of his own shareholders. We tried everything with this guy.

One day one of the folks on my team, Steve Miller (recently the interim CEO of Waste Management), went to see the Rockford banker. Miller called me and said the bank president wouldn't even see him.

Miller's plan was to go sit on the steps of that bank until the president agreed to a meeting.

And that's what Miller did.

The local media came. In front of the cameras, Miller said this bank was the last holdout, and if it didn't agree to the loans, Chrysler was going to die. It turned out to be a good public relations maneuver.

There was a big Chrysler assembly plant in nearby Belvedere, Illinois. A lot of the Chrysler employees saw Miller on television and heard his statement. The next day, they started to close down their accounts in this bank.

By the end of the day, the president of the bank faced the cameras and said he was not going to watch his bank be destroyed.

Reluctantly, he said, I am signing this loan for Chrysler.

And that finished it.

We thought we had it made. But we didn't.

We were all prepared for a big ceremony and news conference in Washington. We were all set up in front of the media. Doug Fraser of the United Auto Workers was there, along with Iacocca and a collection of cabinet members.

Doug Fraser made a famous statement.

"This pay cut contract is the worst contract I have ever negotiated, but it sure beats the alternative."

At the last minute, the government folks said, "Nope. You're not ready. You have to get a formal agreement in Canada."

I looked at Iacocca and he looked at me.

We jumped on an airplane and people started making phone calls. Friday night, we opened negotiations with the Canadians at 10:30 P.M.

A minister of the federal government in Canada said they could agree to the deal only if the Ontario provincial government also took a share in the risk.

The negotiations concluded at 2:00 A.M. Saturday. The deal included one clause that Chrysler would have to agree to research projects that would be paid for by the province of Ontario.

What kind of research projects?

That was up to us.

It was 3:30 A.M.

I called Hal Sperlich, Chrysler's vice president for engineering and product planning at the time.

"I know you are not going to believe this," I said. "But right now you have to help me make up at least four plausible research projects we can do in Ontario and I am going to prepare them as a document."

We fooled around on the phone for two hours and came up with the projects. We called the Ontario government at 10:30 A.M. Saturday and signed the documents.

I woke up Iacocca and we jumped on an airplane and called ahead to Washington announcing that the Canadian federal and provincial governments had said yes. In Washington, they were excited about the prospect of a news conference. But they wanted to wait for us.

Iacocca and I were exhausted.

We poured ourselves a drink on the plane and toasted each other. It was a very emotional moment.

I cried.

We were exhausted and we were not going to go to Washington looking like bums. We went back to Detroit. I went home and climbed into bed.

Two hours later Glenda was listening to the radio. She came in to report really big news for Detroit.

One of its most important companies had been saved.

I cried again.

Getting the loan guarantees wasn't the end of the game.

We needed product and acceptance in the marketplace. That was what would save us or not. We also had to lower our costs, and fast.

We still faced that immediate problem of having just about no cash.

So we created our own interim financing. We told our suppliers we were out of money. We asked them to stake us, to keep shipping parts. By the time we got the first loan guarantees from the federal government, we owed our suppliers $400 million. The next day, we paid them off.

Even as we were trying to save Chrysler, we had to build its business. Lee Iacocca, the pitchman, was at his best. He was on the road to winning the hearts of America. His company was falling apart, but rebuilding trust inside Chrysler and outside in the marketplace was crucial.

I watched Lee selling the K-car.

He really was magnificent.

He could talk you into buying anything, whether you were a banker, or a customer, or an employee.

Obviously the campaign worked. In fact it worked so well that Iacocca was on the list of potential presidential candidates.

The K-car was under development with Sperlich, the genius from Ford, in charge. It was an extraordinarily bold move.

Until then, the American carmakers had focused on big cars with big engines and lots of space, because that is what customers wanted. Customers changed their minds when gasoline prices started to climb.

In the 1970s, coming off the Arab oil embargo and gasoline shortages, people had rushed out to buy diesel VW Rabbits as the price of gasoline climbed to $2 a gallon.

Sperlich and the other product planners at Chrysler believed that the American family car was going to have to get smaller and lighter and have a four-cylinder engine and burn less fuel.

The space inside a car like that would be at a premium, but the car would still have to be roomy to draw family car buyers.

Hal believed you could get maximum internal space and minimum external space with front-wheel drive. His goal was to build the biggest, lightest front-wheel-driven car that could be powered by a four-cylinder engine.

By the time Iacocca showed up at Chrysler, the K-car was already within twelve to fifteen months of production.

Ever the salesman and fully aware that Chrysler needed something to believe in, Iacocca grabbed it.

This is America's new family car, he argued, setting the standard for fuel efficiency.

Washington would love that.

He persuaded car dealers to be patient. He persuaded the suppliers to be patient. He persuaded the banks to be patient.

Then an advertising agency came along and taught us a lesson that should be of significance to every CEO in America.

Ad agencies almost always play to the ego of the chief. In many cases, they will argue that what this product needs, what this company needs, is for the CEO to be the spokesperson in the commercials.

"Look," they will say, "it's all right here in the research."
Run the other way!

When Iacocca started on TV, he was terrible.

He got really good at it later, but that was only what any-one might expect from Iacocca.

Point number two.

When someone with a vested interest says he has the re-search to prove his point, ask who did the research. In most cases, the agency will say it has an excellent research de-partment and does all of its own research.

Respond this way: "From now on, we will have a separate and independent group that does research. We don't like people being their own judges."

The K-car worked.

It was the savior of the company.

True to form, both Sperlich and Iacocca worked their magic. They were masters at taking one hundred parts from the four thousand parts of a car, changing them, and making the product look like another car.

We had a K-car convertible. We had a stretched K-car. We had K-car station wagons.

But then Chrysler hung on to the idea for too long. It ac-cepted the proposition that gas was going to stay at $2 or go higher. That wasn't right. Gasoline prices dropped and stabilized. The American public did not want family cars with four cylinders after a while. We waited for an extra three or four years before we listened to the real world in-stead of listening only to ourselves. We finally designed a new bigger series of V-6 engine cars.

We had another ace, too.

The minivan!

Even looking back today, the minivan was probably the best automotive product in the last three decades. And Hal Sperlich was its champion.

He had actually created the minivan, with Iacocca's sup-port, at Ford. But it just looked too weird, and Ford would never let it get beyond the design phase. Worse than that, every time they went out to do research, they would get a bad response. People just didn't like the way it looked. They would respond, "I wouldn't buy that."

But Hal had the foresight to know that it would work.

There are probably only six people in the world who have the rare skill of being able to look at the mock-up of a car and figure out what the public would want three years later. Hal was one of them, and Iacocca was one of them. Bob Lutz, later at Chrysler, was probably the best of them.

But even Hal had his blind spot.

He couldn't get past thinking that the product was a van. When you think of it as a van, you design it half as a car and half as a truck. Iacocca said no, if this was going to work, the Chrysler minivan was going to have to be a car.

But Hal fought that and said it would have to incorporate a lot of truck design if it was going to be accepted by the federal government as a truck, with fewer regulatory requirements. This fight went on and on.

One day we were looking at side glass in the van. It was truck type glass, indented as opposed to flat car glass across the plane of the outer surface. Hal said, "We can't do this. It will cost another $40 extra per van." We said, "What's another $40."

Multiply $40 by 500,000 vehicles per year, and it's a lot of money.

Three weeks later, we found out what the overall investment cost would be for the minivan. It was going to take $700 million to produce the tools and facilities.

I said, "We don't have the money." Sperlich and I looked at each other. The thought hit us at exactly the same time.

If we don't have the money anyhow, what's another $700 million?

We launched the minivan out of sheer grit.

Our competitors were lost. It took them twelve years to produce minivans that could compete with Chrysler minivans. Every year, they would argue that it just wouldn't succeed or that the trend wouldn't last or that they had a better design.

Once again, people thought I was nuts. I predicted that before the minivan phase was over, worldwide sales would climb to two million vehicles a year. I don't think the number ever got that high, but I was close. I made my prediction early in the process, when we were selling only fifty thousand minivans a year. Sales rocketed.

That was a lesson in the limits of research. Sometimes, research cannot give you the answers, and that creates a tough situation.

There are products and services that the public just can't understand or appreciate in advance, but once they enter the market, they can be enormously successful.

Research is great, but sometimes you have to rely on experience—and your gut instinct.

I had a great eleven-year run at Chrysler.

Ultimately, my responsibilities stretched from Acustar, a $4 billion auto components company with 25,000 employees, to Chrysler Financial Corp., which was a $40 billion business. I was responsible for Chrysler Technologies, which included Gulfstream, the business jet company, and Electronic Systems, Inc., a defense contractor. I was in charge of Chrysler's international activities and I shared with Lee the responsibility of all of Chrysler.

But I never got to run that promised truck division.

Was it hard to leave?

You bet.

An experience like that changes a man, even changes the way he thinks about the passage of time. Some people mark the passage of a year by the arrival of allergy season. They start sniffling or itching and know spring has arrived.

Once a year, I regret no longer being in the car business.

That is when the new models are introduced.

I still have that twinge of excitement about all the new

cars in the industry. We trained the whole season for that day. It was the World Series and you wanted to see all the players on the field.

Sometimes I wonder if I could have run Chrysler better than the people who succeeded Lee.

I think I might have, but I am certainly in the minority in that conclusion. The shareholders are undoubtedly happy that Chrysler sold itself to Daimler-Benz. The management seemed happy, too. They got paid off in big option exercises.

I think the workers at Chrysler will be better off, too, because I suspect Daimler-Benz will add production in the United States, because it costs less to make cars here.

At the same time, it is always better to be the buyer than the seller. I could never have sold Chrysler.

A living, breathing entity has disappeared because of that sale. Two or three years from now, the folks who are the senior management at Chrysler will probably be gone.

But that won't change the fact that the day I walked in, the place was a disaster and that I got to play my part in bringing it back to life and helping it to thrive.

SIX

★

Not Such Friendly Skies

I walked out of Chrysler in Detroit and into Chicago in 1990 for my first shot at helping United's employees buy their airline. It was like walking into a food processor running at the frappé setting.

This was one year after United's CEO, Steve Wolf, and the pilots union had tried to buy the airline. They were proposing $300 a share. That would have created a debt of $6 billion. To my mind, that would have crippled United Airlines.

But there were other problems, too.

The International Association of Machinists and Aerospace Workers was not part of the deal, didn't like it at all, and decided to battle it out with both Wolf and the pilots union. That had already poisoned the atmosphere, and what was revealed in the legal disclosures presented to explain the deal didn't help.

If the sale had gone through, they showed that Steve Wolf would have made millions.

When the pilots discovered that, they got angry at Wolf, too.

So two of United's key unions were bitter, and that bitterness spilled over into some layers of management.

When the United board realized what was happening, it concluded that if the unions could not get along with management, then they ought to buy the company themselves.

All the parties negotiated and came up with a deal. They needed $4 billion and they needed a new CEO to get them going.

That was going to be me.

The three unions that had a chance to buy United wanted me as CEO. The plan was that once the money was available to buy the company, under predetermined terms, I would step in as CEO and Wolf would leave.

I had concluded it was time to say farewell to Chrysler.

It was tough to leave the place because we had all worked so hard to save it, and had done so well at the job over time. I had worked with Lee Iacocca for eleven of the most difficult years of my life, but the rewards were tremendous. We saved a company that seemed doomed in 1979, nursed it back to health, and then built it up to the point at which it was thriving when it was time for me to leave.

It was clear to me that I was not going to be running Chrysler. Iacocca had every intention of staying in the top job for as long as he could. But I was itching to run something. I had built a lifetime's experience in a little more than a decade.

If Chrysler wasn't going to be the mountain I climbed, I would shift my sights elsewhere. I liked the challenge at United, even though I knew going in that it was going to be hard work.

I was accustomed to hard work.

I was ready to give this campaign at United everything I had, because the idea of employee ownership of such a huge company seemed critically important to me. I knew from my years at Ford and Chrysler what happened when workers viewed themselves as being distant, almost disconnected, from the fortunes and failures of their companies.

I was no stranger to trouble after all those years at Chrysler, so I wasn't frightened by what I found at United.

In 1990, United was about to face severe losses as the airline industry went through one of its periodic downturns. Add that to the bitterness between the unions and management, and there wasn't anything friendly at all about the skies over United.

My first job was to arrange the $4 billion in financing that would pay for the 1990 employee purchase.

I had learned my lessons well at Chrysler. There's nothing in the world like having your back pressed so hard to the wall that it seems you are merging with the paint. That had been the story of my first difficult years working with Iacocca.

I knew that one way to get the cash we needed to buy United would be to construct a consortium of bankers, employees, and suppliers. But I also knew I would need a good team to help me through the struggle.

It is never much fun to move into such a bitter situation, but my immediate role was to be the conquering hero, the next CEO. It is rare that a CEO gets that kind of an opportunity, to work quietly without portfolio so that you can get everything in place, ready for your move into the front office.

I put together a small team of people.

John Edwardson was the most important. He was my financial adviser.

Edwardson was rock-solid. He had been one of the top three people in a smaller conglomerate and had four years of experience as chief financial officer at Northwest Airlines.

We created a shadow management for the company, with the agreement that he, too, would work behind the scenes and then step into the CFO's job when I became CEO.

We had to build that shadow management structure because we knew that once we had the financing lined up, and once we had closed on the deal, United would be our company to run.

I couldn't ignore Steve Wolf, but I must say that our conversations through that period were businesslike and to the point, in the extreme. There was no male bonding in that situation, no glue in the relationship.

But shadow managing was crucial. The last thing United needed was a new CEO and financial team that had to spend six months to a year learning where the coat racks were and how the place actually operated. We would be $4 billion in debt, loaded with commitments to bankers and suppliers, and facing great expectations from employees.

We would be competing in one of the hottest and most complicated businesses on earth. United had operating profit losses, but a positive cash flow. It was fighting head to head with American and Delta for the number one position in total sales. It was viewed as mediocre at best with regard to passenger service. It needed to replenish its fleet. And it wasn't growing very quickly.

I believed, and the banks believed, that United had the capability of managing its debt through a combination of cash flow and the selective sale of some noncore assets. If we could just get started, we thought we would be okay because we were going to lower the operating costs of the company through deep labor savings. The employees were going to be taking a pay cut to buy their shares of stock, and that would be a tremendous help.

Because that was our plan, we had to find a way to know what was really going on inside the airline. We had to know what assets at United were not working, what we might want to sell off. The company was also getting ready to place a major order for new airplanes, and we needed to know all about that, too.

A shadow management team was the way to do it.

There was a deeper reason for shadow management.

There were lingering doubts about whether the old management team at United was happy with the thought of an airline that would be owned by its employees. Would they cooperate with that process, or would they make decisions and operate in a way that might jeopardize the plan? We had to build our own understanding about what was going on instead of accepting the perspectives of the old management team.

Shadow management is a bizarre place.

I had an office at United. But I didn't know what to do with it. I would show up from time to time for meetings, but Steve Wolf didn't want me around. Who would? It would be like having the future sitting right there with you in the room, and recognizing every time I smiled or tried to contribute that you were a part of what would soon be the distant past.

My shadow world title: CEO-in-waiting.

I created that myself.

I thought, what the heck, we have to have a little fun with this.

We started working with a group of bankers who were willing to lend us some or most of the $4 billion. Bankers Trust was very positive. Citicorp wasn't. United had been down this road before. Citicorp had been the lead bank when the pilots and Wolf tried to buy the airline in 1989. Given the $6 billion price tag, we were all fortunate that deal had collapsed.

We faced a thorny challenge right up front on the question of governance. This was a deep reflection of the status of the folks who have the money in the United States versus the workers of America.

The banks wanted to know what would happen in an economic downturn if the company needed to sell assets or lay off people. Could an employee-owned company do that?

I told them that we would do that because we were owners, and we would know we had to.

I was being naive.

The bankers said that was not good enough. They wanted a completely independent board of directors. The unions hesitated. Out of that grew a negotiated structure between the banks and the unions, with me as the honest broker.

No one had ever done anything like this on such a huge scale before. Good boards of directors always reflect the interests of their constituencies, but those constituencies don't always include union activists, strongly independent and meticulous pilots, and machinists steeped in blue-collar traditions.

That governance broke new frontiers.

It was the first time in history that an employee-owned company was seeking so much money from banks. As time went by, the conflicts of interest built into the idea became quite clear.

The unions started on the assumption that if the employees were going to own the airline, they should control the board of directors. The bankers, of course, didn't see it that way. If they were going to advance so much money, they wanted assurances that the board of directors would keep creditors high on the agenda, too.

We had to find a way to balance those conflicts.

Guided by Stuart Oran, now at United but the outside counsel to the pilots union at the time, we hammered out a governance agreement that struck a balance between those competing interests.

We tried to give employees authority to make decisions about issues that concerned them the most. They were worried about some recent history. They charged that previous management had pushed for pay cuts, then took that money and bought rental car companies and hotels. So we wrote in a provision that the employees would have the right to reject acquisitions outside the airline industry. They could also reject asset sales that were not tied to the economic needs of the company. They could also reject major acquisitions of other airlines.

There were different issues at work on the banking side.

The banks wanted to know that United would have a good board of directors and a good chief executive officer who would be free to run the company. Under the governance agreement, we gave the employees the right to reject a proposed CEO, but not the right to pick one.

We told the banks that the majority of the board members would be independent. But the banks were still wary. How did they know we would pick good independent directors? Okay, we said, before you lend us the money, we will announce the names of the new board members.

That sent me on a wild chase to find a good board.

I hired Tom Neff of Spencer Stuart and the two of us signed up a full board of directors. From a standing start, we completed the task in just sixty days. Paul Volcker, former chairman of the Federal Reserve, was one of the selections. Don Perkins, on the Time Warner board among others and the man who had turned the old Jewel Tea Co. into a huge success in Chicago, was another.

The final governance agreement complied with Delaware law for corporate structures, and it satisfied the interests of the banks as creditors and the interests of the unions. We considered that an historic achievement.

The terms were important, and I believe they present a strong lesson in how issues of employee ownership can be negotiated. They were cast fully recognizing that a collection of people who frequently had competing interests would be on the new board.

The agreement provided for a heavyweight independent board of directors, but the employees would have certain veto rights. As previously agreed, the company couldn't run off and acquire other companies without employee approval.

The company could not capriciously cut employment.

It had to have an independent judgment that conditions were clearly in decline before those kinds of measures could be taken. There were also rules on selection of a CEO (which would come into play when it came time to deal with my replacement). There would be union members on the board and on the compensation committee of the board.

We had created the world's first template for balancing

the powers and interests of employees and lenders, even as we met the stiff requirements of Delaware law.

I still view the process as fascinating. It was a precursor of how these issues will be handled in the future, when I hope employee ownership becomes more common.

The business didn't stop as we were trying to resolve the issues of financing and ownership. United was on the verge of making a major purchase of aircraft and engines, which ultimately became the 777. We were a very big airline, so the industry was watching.

I saw an opportunity. Suppliers are crucial to companies in trouble. They have a strong interest in helping a company survive, because their business is so closely tied to the company's success.

I went to the potential aircraft and engine suppliers and I said, "Look, if you will help us buy this company, I will make sure you get the order, assuming equal prices and terms."

It was dicey.

I didn't intend to, but I put them in a very difficult position. The top management that was in place at United may not have wanted the deal to go through. That management could have penalized any of these folks who cooperated with the CEO-in-waiting, the shadow boss, me, if the deal didn't go through.

I played it straight with the suppliers.

I told them exactly what the condition was. Some of them were members of the boards of banks, so they had their own line of information on what was happening.

In the end, it came down to one of those situations where the acquisition plan would work if everyone walked through the door at the same time. The suppliers were saying they liked the idea, but they wanted to be certain that everything would fall into place before they signed the deal. And the banks said they didn't want to commit to the money unless they knew the other part of the arrangement was going to happen.

Sitting there in the late fall of 1990, just a few months after I started working on the United challenge, we had nearly achieved the impossible.

We had all but brought together a variety of differently motivated and sometimes hostile interests, got them facing in the same direction, and made possible the closing of a huge and historic deal.

Then something awful happened.

It was January 16, 1991.

President George Bush's press secretary, Marlin Fitzwater, was on television.

"The liberation of Kuwait has begun," he announced.

Operation Desert Storm.

I didn't know it at the time, but some of the banks were getting a little nervous about their own balance sheets. It had nothing to do with airlines and everything to do with banking. But when Desert Storm happened, the banks got really scared.

Within three days of the start of Desert Storm, the banks showed reluctance. I made my arguments about fuel prices and how history shows oil prices don't just rocket to $30 a barrel and stay there permanently. I told them it would all be over in Kuwait soon enough. I argued they could just view it as a bad year—Right!

But Desert Storm affected more than oil prices.

It made the public scared about travel. And it triggered a recession in the airline industry. At the very moment that too many new aircraft were being delivered, demand dropped and there was too much capacity.

The banks were right, but for the wrong reasons.

And I was right about oil, but not about the recession.

If I had succeeded in that deal, as CEO twenty-four months later I would have had to face cutting back to keep the airline going, a potential crisis for a company just starting the experiment of employee ownership.

I didn't realize right away that it was over, that my first attempt at a United landing had failed. I kept right on trying, fearful but determined.

I went to GE. I told them, "Look, you have GE capital and you've got GE engines. How about we make a deal? GE capital will provide us $1 billion and I'll commit to using GE engines." They took a serious look, but in the end, GE passed.

I went to Marvin Davis. He had always been a man of very big ideas and fearless in business.

Big Marvin, six foot six and struggling with his weight.

He had been a raider against United in 1988. I went to his office in southern California. The first thing he wanted to know was "What do you want for lunch?" Among many other things, he owned a deli. So he brought up what looked like enough food for thirty people. I nibbled and he ate—he ate a lot. He was looking for a way, with extraordinary leverage, to own the majority shares of United.

The union folks were having none of that.

An Austrian showed up, young, confident, and suave.

Lots of money, too. He said he would buy $300 million of the equity. I met him in New York. He was a little vague about where all of the money came from, but he was spreading a lot of it around New York at charity events. I had a gut feeling about all of this, so I backed away.

I didn't want money when I wasn't certain of its source. That is an important business lesson.

It finally dawned on me that this round was over.

I was not going to be CEO of United.

In fact, I was through.

I have a deeply held view about these kinds of setbacks. They are like losing a longtime family pet. I say to myself, "Okay, buster, you get ten days. Go mourn and then figure out what you are going to do next." Everything looked black, everything colorless. Food didn't taste good. I was in deep mourning.

That part is about me. There was a larger issue, too.

Employee ownership appealed to me because it repre-

sented something new and something no one was quite
ready for. To me, those are the two central requirements
for success. You can't just do something better than someone else is already doing it. You have to create something
totally new, maybe something people don't even realize
they want yet.

I ranked employee ownership right up with three other
developments in my lifetime that fit the same standards:
Chrysler's development of the minivan, the founding of
Cable News Network, and the creation of America Online.
All three are examples of a service or a product that someone created before the public knew it wanted it. They
made individuals and shareholders very wealthy.

Employee ownership had, and has, the same potential, I
believe. In 1990, it was, indeed, a deep loss to be mourned.

I had plenty of money, because the United package protected me in the event the deal failed. Much later, Iacocca
and I were getting along again and I was being considered
for CEO at Chrysler. The board was reluctant because I
had been disloyal. I had quit.

Always the genius with the one-liner, Iacocca said, "How
could you blame him. Wouldn't you go if you got an offer
for a $9 million summer job?"

John Edwardson, my financial adviser for the United
deal, and I were hanging out.

I was too young to retire. But I felt I was history. John decided to return to Chicago to spend six months with his
family. He enjoyed it. I thought that was extraordinary and
I admired him a lot for it.

I went to my home in Aspen with Glenda.

We had a delightful time. But I was jittery. Three months
in Aspen and I was ready to jump at about any job offer. I
had a chance to run the Resolution Trust Corp., the salvage agency in the savings and loan collapse. There was a
suggestion that I should run the U.S. Postal Service.

What evolved was a three-year period of extended education that carried me everywhere from investment bank-

ing to truck building in the Czech Republic. It was an extraordinary series of experiences that I view now as valuable side trips on my way back to United.

John Birkelund, a fellow Princeton alum, invited me to become an investment banker. I went to Dillon Read as a managing director.

In retrospect, I was in one of my bouncing-around periods. Type A characters never sit quietly for long. Dillon Read led to Olympia & York, which then led to Tatra in the Czech Republic, where I was wrestling with the legacy of communism and trying to convince a reluctant workforce that having internal auditors did not mean we were bringing in the KGB to bust heads.

I was struggling with all of this when a call came.

September 14, 1993.

"Are you sitting?"

It was Stuart Oran, the bright, young, and energetic lawyer from Paul, Weiss, the New York law firm that was representing the pilots union at United.

Rumors of the death of the employee purchase of United, it seemed, were greatly exaggerated.

Of course I still had my memories of United, the work Oran and I had done trying to get the first deal accomplished, and my CEO-in-waiting days.

I thought of it as opportunity lost. Ideas like employee ownership of an enormous airline don't come along every day. It could only happen once in a lifetime.

But I was wrong.

It was a good thing I was sitting, because I really would have fallen over. The employee purchase deal was alive and they wanted me back to make it run.

The economic situation was worse than it was in 1990. There was a recession and the airline industry was paying a high price. It had too much capacity, too many empty seats, and that problem had so damaged United Airlines that the employees were facing an ultimatum.

Steve Wolf told the employees they should either buy the company, or he would shrink it.

Shrinking meant layoffs.

There was a plan on the table and it didn't require the heavy bank financing that caused such trouble the first time I tried to help the employees buy the company. But it wasn't for a 100 percent buyout. I worked for six months to finalize the deal this time around, and even at that, it barely succeeded. Overriding all the technical and structural issues, there was deep animosity between Wolf and the pilots union.

There were major differences between the first attempt for an employee purchase and the new plan. This time around, the employees would be buying only 55 percent of the company. The flight attendants, a bit reluctant in the first bid, were not going to be part of the agreement this time.

The new plan was on the table as the airline industry was in dire straits.

United alone was looking at a $1 billion annual loss.

That was what drove the new, 1994 employee purchase plan. United had to lower its costs, either by shrinking or by selling itself to its workers.

I never doubted I wanted to take this assignment. It was unfinished business for me, though I never dreamed I would have another chance.

Glenda and I talked about it. I could tell she would have preferred I pass, because taking the job meant postponing retirement. It might involve a move to Chicago, too, to take a job that would put me in the center of a boiling pot full of stress.

But I could only see the challenge, the excitement, the personal opportunity to play in the World Series again, to test myself as CEO in a major company in a new industry for me. And of course, majority employee ownership would put me to the biggest of tests.

Glenda was great about endorsing my plans and she set

out to build a new home for us in Colorado for our retirement. Taking the United job would probably postpone that retirement date for five years.

I was the facilitator for this deal. There were a lot of issues on the table, among them deciding which managers would be replaced, fee levels for advisers, last-minute corporate governance questions, noncompete clauses for departing executives, and efforts to develop a package for the Association of Flight Attendants to join the ownership group.

I was negotiating my own compensation, too.

That was quite an experience; the pilots and the machinists unions had a lot of learning to do about compensation for CEOs.

There was some irony at work in the compensation negotiations.

The union heads and I were in clear agreement that there is too big a gap between compensation of CEOs and workers. But my answer to that problem was that no single company could solve it alone without taking undue risk.

If United chose to pay its new management below market rates, then the best of the managers would be easy pickings for other airlines or other companies. The unions agreed intellectually, but they were still struggling with how to deal with the concerns, doubts, and complaints of their members about executive salaries.

Beneath the philosophy, there was another reality at work.

Compensation for CEOs, in addition to being high and big, is very complicated business. A worker gets base pay, maybe an incentive bonus, and some benefits. But CEOs have their compensation constructed so that it ties into shareholder value, and there can be a lot of elements in that formula. Bonuses for performance are involved, as well as stock options, and whether those options are pegged at current market prices or higher. That means they only have value if the market price rises.

How do you put a value on that kind of compensation?

The existing board and management insisted on staying out of my compensation discussions. Ultimately, my contract was endorsed by the new board the first day we convened as an employee-owned company.

I hired a very good compensation attorney.

The unions matched him with about twenty to thirty lawyers, most of them labor lawyers. It took three months to get a contract completed. The old board wanted clean hands. I was, for the moment, the unions' choice and the unions' person, although from day one I insisted the agreement could only work if everyone recognized I was the CEO of all the shareholders, employee and public.

My annual salary would be $725,000 less 8 percent (my part of the salary cut to buy shares in the company). There would also be a performance bonus I could earn of $725,000, restricted stock, and options to buy United stock.

As part of the deal, Steve Wolf and his two key team members would be leaving. I had to find a president and an executive vice president even as I was carving out my own arrangement and trying to help the employees with the purchase of the total company.

I had to spend a lot of my time reassuring the pilots that employee ownership was the right choice.

At one point, the stock dropped and the pilots insisted on reworking the deal. The whole ownership plan almost came undone. There was a modest change in the deal, and we moved on.

The pilots and the machinists would have to take a pay cut to buy their ownership and this was unnerving to them, even though they would be getting 55 percent of United in return. For the pilots, that meant giving up 23 percent of a salary that averaged about $130,000 a year. Was this a concessionary contract, or an investment to buy majority ownership of their company?

Everyone didn't get the same level of pay cut.

The goal was to cut salaries enough to buy the stock for

the employees to own 55 percent of the company. The pilots made up only 8,000 of United's 76,000 employees at the time, but they took the deepest cut and got the biggest share of the company. The machinists took less of a cut and got a smaller share, salaried and management people took modest cuts and got the smallest share, and the flight attendants decided they did not want to participate. They took no salary cuts and got no share of the company.

The argument was that over the long term, salaries would be restored and everyone would fare well as the airline prospered. But that kind of formula required trust, something that was in very short supply at United.

In the end, the International Association of Machinists approved the deal by a narrow 56 percent, and that was only because the unionized kitchen workers, who were going to be laid off because of outsourcing, were given the chance to be included in the vote. Their incentive was a liberal severance package if the ownership deal went forward and a poor package if it collapsed.

There was turmoil in the pilots union, too. The union took a straw poll, but no formal membership vote. The pilots union leadership was thrown out and replaced by new leaders right after the deal closed. The new candidates campaigned for their jobs with the promise that all future matters of importance would require a formal membership ratification vote.

I am still not quite sure why the flight attendants didn't participate, but I suspect they were looking for excuses to say no because they did not want to take a pay cut. They found a reason when I said I would not close all the foreign flight attendant bases. I could not imagine telling eight hundred foreign employees they would be losing their jobs, not out of economic necessity, but because of an agreement between new management and their own flight attendants union.

In the run-up to the shareholder vote to approve employee ownership and for a few months after, I spent about 80 percent of my time holding town hall meetings with employees to talk about my future plans for the company. I also wanted to hear their needs and wants.

A lot has been written over the years about "walk around" management. I was "walking around" the world in this new role, listening to the complaints and dreams of United's employees and formulating a plan for the company at the same time.

On the surface, I kept hearing that everyone wanted liberalized flying passes and better internal communication. That sounded simple enough to me, but one of the union leaders said I shouldn't touch the question of passes. It was too emotional. He suggested the issue be handed to a committee of employees. That was when I learned how hot the issue is among airline folks. For a lot of them, it is why they work for an airline—free standby passes anywhere the airline flies.

Employees care about the type of pass they receive—priority for standby, which family members are included, payment amounts, arrangements for disabled employees, arrangements for retirees, the frequency they can fly.

The debates over these terms are never-ending.

I have since concluded that there is no such thing as a policy on passes that all airline employees will like. United has had one of the most liberal policies in the industry, and some people still aren't happy with it.

The unhappiness went deeper than questions of passes and communications.

There was distrust that had come out of the employees' experience with management.

A lot of people were unhappy that the flight attendants had not come in as owners. They thought they were getting a free ride. There were many concerns that United did not have a clear direction. What were we going to be and where were we headed?

People were angry that their company seemed to be intent on copying whatever American Airlines did. Didn't we have the intelligence and courage to plot our own course? It became a drumbeat: "Why are we always following American's lead?" They cited frequent flyer programs, advertising, and a whole range of business issues that had led the workers to conclude United was a follower, not a leader, in the airline industry.

There were also doubts about whether United's old management, particularly middle management, could learn new ways to work with employee owners.

They were also afraid of the question of outsourcing, even though the contract allowing employees to buy stock included the right for management to outsource some of the work.

Communication was a different matter.

I looked back over my own career and realized that, in hard times, the two areas that seemed to be slashed first by management were internal communication and employee training costs.

That seemed wrong to me.

Ask yourself this question: How is it that senior corporate managers claim that people are their most important asset, and yet training of people, and communicating with people, are the first programs to get tossed when a recession hits?

Improved internal communication was one of my first assignments. Thank goodness I spent the first two or three months on the job holding those town hall meetings with United employees all over the world. It helped me decide where I wanted to take the company and it helped the employees understand and know me and my ideas.

What emerged from those sessions was an important realization: United did not have a strategic long-term plan.

We were not alone. Best I could tell, no airline had a strategic plan. How can you get everyone going in the same direction if you have no strategic plan? That is not a rhetorical question.

The answer is you can't.

The rationalization behind the lack of a plan was that the airline industry changes so quickly, and so radically, that by the time there is a strategic plan on paper, it's obsolete. I didn't buy it. I thought they were hiding behind the sluggish attitude that there was just no use in planning in a world that changes so rapidly.

It was my intention to create a plan we could live with, then refine it and update it as we moved along.

One of our first moves was to establish a much healthier fleet plan, which would identify which aircraft would be replaced and what kind of planes we would purchase given our markets. We wanted Boeing 747s and 777s and Airbus 320s and 319s. The Boeings were long-distance, efficient airplanes that would allow us to fly throughout the world. We chose Airbus 319s and 320s for inside-the-U.S. flying and because they are very passenger-friendly.

Fleet planning and schedule making are complicated business, but United has a collection of very smart people who help make those decisions. They are very aggressive thinkers and doers.

I recall the day one of them came to me and told me United should purchase one of IBM's Big Blue computers, the same model that beat the Russian grand master at chess. It was the only computer big enough to crunch all the potential permutations and deliver profitable airline schedules, I was told.

We bought the machine.

It was very complicated. It screwed up for one full quarter and it cost us $25 million. Then we adjusted it, learned how to use it, and made a lot of money.

Setting up a more realistic fleet plan also gave our maintenance people the opportunity to lay out a sensible, stable maintenance plan. They would know better which airplanes would be coming into bases for maintenance, how many people would be needed, and how much inventory they would have to keep on hand.

We established some goals for productivity, too. We wanted to grow the number of employees at a slower rate than the growth pace of the airline, without causing people to work harder. We had efficiency plans in the works.

The financial plan was crucial. We decided we were going to set out to create the cash first for investment-grade credit ratings, then create enough cash to buy new planes to replace the old ones, and finally enough cash to buy new planes to expand the size of the fleet.

We stopped right there in the first plan, but amended the financial road map later to add another goal, giving returns back to our shareholders through dividends and stock buybacks.

We thought our way through what it was going to take for the outside financial world to respect us. We wanted Wall Street to view employee ownership as good for all shareholders, not as a threat to outside investors.

We said we wanted to achieve double-digit growth in earnings per share, year after year, in normal times.

(As of mid-1999, we had four years of double-digit growth earnings and in 1998, a recession year in Asia, we still achieved single-digit earnings per share growth. Our stock price had about tripled.)

We also launched a whole series of multiyear cost initiatives aimed at constantly trying to improve our profits.

A lot of them are competitive measures, so I am not going to tell you what they are. But one of our cost initiatives was aimed at reducing spare parts inventory. We unleashed teams on the problem to find more modern ways to manage parts. That might sound mundane until you realize that parts inventory amounts to a lot of money sitting in place and doing nothing. The idea was to have what you need where you need it, not to have everything you might need sitting in storage gathering dust.

We attacked the question of taxes, too.

United probably fills out three thousand tax forms a

year, an extraordinary administrative burden. We wanted
to find ways to reduce property and inventory taxes.

During the strategic plan process, I learned that at
United, as at many companies, management had been in-
tensely focused on controlling and containing labor costs.
That is important, of course, but it overlooks the fact that
at an airline, and probably in many other companies, only
a third of the total cost of operation is in labor.

So why spend 100 percent of your management time focusing on 33 percent of your costs, especially in an area
that is so fraught with emotion? You could be spending a
lot more time on the other 67 percent of that cost structure. You make a lot more progress that way, and it is much
easier to get everyone to help if you are not focusing on
pay or job reductions.

In 1998, United had about $17 billion in revenue and
made about $2 billion in profits. That meant the $15 billion left covered costs, with a third of that amount covering
people and the rest paying for everything else.

Look at it this way. If you take out salaries, benefits, and
all of the components you need to support them, what is
left is the physical part of the airline, 67 percent of your
costs.

Distribution costs alone at United amounted to $2.7 bil-
lion a year. These are the costs for passengers to book on
United and pay us. They include travel agent commissions,
reservations system costs, telephone call costs, credit card
costs, and software fee charges.

When I left United in 1999, we were on track to take $1
billion a year out of those distribution costs, and wring a lot
of hassle out of the process for the flying public, primarily
by using technology.

United spends $2 billion a year on fuel. We put a team
on that issue, too. The company was already astute about
the purchase of fuel. It would buy forward, hedging its bets
by buying at low prices where possible, or shift its purchases
around the world. But there were other savings available.

Auxiliary power units, the engines that provide electricity for the planes when they are on the ground, were being used too often. We also found ways to cut fuel use during taxiing.

We reviewed all of our leases and ground maintenance costs.

Looking back, it's a pretty good record. I walked into an airline that had lost $1 billion. A lot of people seemed to hate each other on a very personal basis. I walked out of a company that was making $2 billion a year in profit and that was more than half owned by its employees.

Not bad.

But the numbers only tell part of the story of what happens when employees become owners.

SEVEN

★

Workers Paradise?

Employee ownership."

It has a nice ring to it, doesn't it?

It conjures up images of happy workers marching toward a common goal, treating one another decently and honestly. They will spread colorful blankets on the lawn in the summer and have Socratic sessions aimed at solving problems. It is socialist art come to life, tractor makers and administrators and big, muscled workers all pushing toward the same goal in a spirit of equality and mutual respect.

In your fondest dreams.

What the idea runs into immediately is culture.

For me, culture in a company means, "How we work and interact, all 100,000 of us, to satisfy customers and earn a profit."

The culture of a company doesn't change overnight, no matter who owns it. Culture has been created over a long period of time and involves a mix of old slights, relationships, and business practices that simply happened, without much thought.

We saw that kind of cultural problem playing out last summer, 2000, as United's pilots, working without a contract, refused to take overtime assignments. The entire system slowed down, thousands of people missed their flights, the airline's good reputation seemed to sour almost overnight.

To my mind, United and its employees had broken one

of the Ten Commandments of Business. They were unable to settle their problems without hurting their customers. I would think that when the dust settles, they will all want to do a postmortem and ask themselves how they can avoid this sort of thing the next time around. If they can answer that question, they can be back on a positive road for employee ownership.

My fear is that this experience will bring into question the value of employee ownership.

It shouldn't. A lot of good ideas have died for the wrong reason. The lesson in this experience is that labor contracts should run for longer periods of time and they should include profit-sharing incentives that increase salaries as a company's profits increase. The labor side should recognize that its role has changed, too, and that unions have as great an interest in keeping customers happy as shareholders and managers have.

But old habits die hard. You can't just stamp "Employee Owned" on a company and expect everything to work out.

I always believed it was a good idea for everybody to get to know one another. That sounds simple, doesn't it? Okay, here is your challenge (actually, it was my challenge, too): Find a way to get union guys and management guys to socialize together.

What I found is that the culture at work in United would not even allow union officials to play golf with management people, because the union folks were afraid that would be seen as compromising their independence, or as being co-opted by management.

There were some revealing cultural incidents, too.

The head of the pilots union and I got along quite well, and occasionally we would end up coming back to Chicago after a meeting on the same plane. Both of us would always make a point of going to the cockpit to talk to the pilots. But the union leader always felt the need to make it clear that it was just a coincidence that we were both on the same plane.

On a broader level, there was a feeling among the employees that they had heard all the happy talk of management before, and that this new call for change was just an echo of stale management gab from previous leaders.

What evolved from that attitude was this conclusion, which I ran into many times in my travels around United: When my boss changes, then I will start to change.

At every layer of the company, it was the same, "You change first and then I will consider it."

And in some cases, people wanted their bosses to change and those who worked beneath them to change, and then they would consider changing themselves.

I believed all of this came from well-intentioned but badly executed previous efforts.

The governance restrictions themselves were good examples of the problem. There were such deep feelings of distrust within the company that all sorts of commitments and balances of power had to be put in concrete in the structure of the company itself.

Employee ownership in any company is not an end. It is just a beginning.

It changes the framework in which you negotiate. But it doesn't change the issues that face companies every day.

One of my big disappointments at United was a belief that if we offered job security, meaning no layoffs, there would be a change in employee behavior—less interest in protecting jobs, much more interest in productivity.

We would only resort to layoffs in the face of a deep recession. I thought this commitment, linked to employee ownership, would change the atmosphere at United.

It helped.

But it didn't change the culture, primarily because of old habits in the unions and lack of trust among employees.

In the beginning, there was some moderate acceptance of outsourcing of work. We wanted to do what we do best and outsource other activities.

We would bring in work from other airlines if we could profit and that would add jobs. But to date, the fear of outsourcing remains. We have not yet fundamentally changed the way employees work or think about their company.

I think we have come around as managers. We offer better training for our people, better internal communications, and better recruiting. But we have a long way to go.

We still need to get better at selecting our first- and second-line management, and we need to get a lot better at supporting these folks so they can learn how to direct and motivate their employees in a modern way. We don't want to give up accountability.

I know it seems like a highlight on the obvious, but it is something that must be underlined in employee-owned companies: Supervisors are responsible for the performance of their people. Every day we deal with the awkward balance of rights versus responsibilities of employees who are employee owners.

That doesn't mean supervisors can behave the way they behaved at Ford in the 1950s and 1960s, or sometimes at Chrysler, or sometimes at United before I had arrived.

I told them all that the day when you could supervise with a two-by-four was over. Shouting at employees and treating them as serfs won't work in an employee-owned company, particularly in an employee-owned company in an era in which workers can simply shift companies if they don't like the conditions.

I told them they had to become coaches and leaders and that they had to abandon the role of tough, screaming bosses. Bully-bossing is over.

I thought I was being quite clear; but I made a big mess for a while.

Some supervisors concluded, "Oh, I get it. If I criticize one of my people and he writes a letter to Greenwald, then I'm in trouble." It was a good lesson for me. You can't just go out and tell people they are expected to supervise differently. You have to put them through some training to help with that, which is exactly what we did at United. Miss that step and the likely response will be, "Okay, I'm not going to manage my people anymore."

We taught supervisors some basic skills about handling people. They seem remarkably simple, but they are exactly the kinds of things that many people forget when they get into supervisory positions.

We suggested that they begin every workday with a five- or ten-minute conversation with their people to talk about what they were going to do that day and about the mistakes they had made the day before.

For example, it's easy to track when there is a serious lag time in getting jetways to airplanes. Miss the timing target on the moving jetways and your customers are going to spend a couple of extra minutes standing on the plane waiting for the door to open. Frequent travelers know what that is like: a computer on one shoulder, a suit bag on the other, and everyone crammed into the aisle. It makes for unhappy customers.

Begin the day with a conversation about how important it is to get the customer off the plane on time, and that problem can be solved.

We also taught our supervisors that there is no such thing as a dumb question. They are obliged to answer all of them. And if they don't have the answer, they are allowed to say, "I don't know, but I will find out." Then they have to go find the answer.

In the old days, they would have made something up.

We taught employees how to build task teams, too, that cut across various functions. It was a way to guide them toward greater efficiency, and it also taught them how to solve their own problems.

There were other issues, as well.

Some of our early employee surveys told us, for example, that employee owners felt they had the right to come to work late and leave early. We had a tough time with this problem, particularly in some of our bigger population centers where we still have time cards.

Most American companies have gotten away from time cards. They depend on supervisors to track attendance. But there are some United sites where the population is so big and so spread out geographically that the supervisor can't do that. We had hoped we could count on a sense of responsibility to get employee owners to work on time and spend the full day on the job. But we were disappointed.

I think a lot of those questions center, again, on the issue of culture. That is one of the most significant changes at United Airlines. We knew we had to get people to think, from top to bottom, as owners. It wasn't just a place they came to work every day. It was their place, their responsibility.

I have never worked with a better collection of officers. It wasn't easy to build that team. A few officers who couldn't sign on had to leave.

Now we have a team that doesn't back-stab. Officers don't climb over one another in their quest for personal success. They work together with the deep-felt belief that contributing to the company and working together as a team will deliver better results for them as individuals.

But United still has a lot of work to do, particularly in the first, second, and third layers of supervision and management. For employees to feel comfortable about taking responsibility and the power that comes with it, someone has to give something up. That feeling is very uncomfortable for supervisors. They have to learn that their own power is enhanced when they give authority to the people who work for them.

The need for cultural change is apparent within the unions, too.

Early on, John Edwardson, then president and COO, was talking to the pilots union council, and one of them came up with a revealing, novel idea.

Now that we are owners, he said, don't you think we ought to be able to fire one officer every twelve months, you know, just get one of them out?

Well, John responded, the officers are now owners of the

company, too. Should they be allowed to pick one pilots union official every twelve months and fire him? That sounds like one of those cute management stories, but it happened. It really got everyone to think much more clearly about the meaning of employee ownership—not just rights, but responsibilities, too.

I don't want to be too critical of our efforts to change the culture. There are many, many signs that United's employees are grasping their new responsibilities and taking them seriously.

I measured that progress over time as I held my town hall meetings around the company. When I first started holding those sessions, about 80 percent of the questions amounted to this: "What are you going to do for me now that I am an owner?" About halfway through my five years as CEO, that began to change. People would pop up to announce they had a good idea for the company that no one was listening to, or they would ask astute questions about the company's profits.

Going through our strategic plan with employees, talking about it in town hall meetings, publicizing it in communications, all of that helped employees understand and know where we were going and how we were going to get there.

We tried a lot of experiments aimed at reducing supervision.

Today there are some parts of United that have zero supervision. The employees looked at their situation and concluded they didn't need another layer of supervision. They stepped up and took responsibility for their own jobs. If you stopped into one of our service areas at midnight, where the task of the night is tire repair, you would find no supervisors, just employees repairing airplane tires.

You are going to know fairly quickly if they aren't doing their jobs, because the maintenance crews will be searching without luck for fresh aircraft tires. But that hasn't happened.

Even though we have had differences, we have been able

to talk them through with the unions without spilling our problems over on the flying public. In my five years at United, I have seen the ugly side of union-management problems at other airlines spill over onto the passengers.

There was a midterm pay increase that was part of our stock purchase package, for example. A real difference of opinion developed over that issue and some anger surfaced.

The agreement that created employee ownership said that in the first five years there would be an opportunity for two pay increases of up to 5 percent each, but that the increases would have to be determined by how well the company was doing.

I came away concluding there should be two pay increases of 3 percent based on that measure, arguing that we would put in profit-sharing benefits and they would carry us to 5 percent if we did well.

All hell broke loose.

The employees viewed that decision as evidence that management was failing the test of employee ownership. That led to a demand that at the end of the five-year period, pay would be at least equal to what it had been before concessions to buy stock. We debated this question for three months.

In the interim, one of those wonderful business miracles happened. Profitability improved so strongly that we were able to go all the way to 5 percent and agree to the "snapback" at the end of five years. I had built a modicum of goodwill, and when we took that last step, everyone was satisfied.

The important point was that we got past the problem. We were able to put the new midterm pay increases into effect without lasting animosity among us, and it never affected our passengers.

The employee ownership plan is straightforward. Take stock in exchange for salary cuts. That is what the United employees agreed to: long-term gain in exchange for short-term sacrifice.

The problem is that old behavior roars back onto the scene at contract time, particularly if a company is doing well. Over the past summer, the pilots' showdown at United was a reflection of the fact that a lot of people still don't realize that their roles have changed. They didn't go on strike, but they did slap themselves in the face by damaging relationships with customers. It seemed to me that they were overlooking what they stood to gain over the long term.

Despite all the trouble, there was a silver lining to this big customer service cloud. In 1998 the pilots and I agreed that an ideal situation would be a new contract that took over a day after the old one ended. Of course, they missed that mark in April 2000. But they did get a tentative settlement in August, which is good given the historical fact that airline union negotiations generally take forever. Given that track record, they came remarkably close.

My argument had always been that it was an investment. My pitch was simple: You are going to buy stock anyway through your savings program. If you do that the typical way, you will earn your salary, send some tax money to Uncle Sam, and then start saving.

Many have become cynical about employee ownership because it has often been misused.

I told them employee ownership would give them a chance to cut Uncle Sam out of the formula, as they would be getting stock in exchange for untaxed salary.

Employee ownership presents a more difficult challenge when a company is a half step from the grave. The cuts in pay don't produce enough cash fast enough and the company still doesn't make it despite the efforts of its employees.

As a result, employees, particularly in the airline industry, tell stories about stock at Pan Am and Eastern, all of which ultimately became worthless.

There are also cases in which American managers believe that once employees become owners, everything will change dramatically. They expect a new dawn when everyone arrives for work that first Monday morning.

Believe me. It doesn't happen.

Employee ownership gave United some very important advantages. The biggest one was that our employees were certainly ready for change; they even demanded change, even if they didn't quite know what changes they wanted.

They were tired of being followers in the airline industry. They were tired of hearing about company losses. They were tired of command and control management style. They were tired of the ongoing fights between unions and management.

That gave us a fast start to shift power down to the employees, particularly those who were working directly with customers.

There were some pretty naive ideas at the beginning.

Some people thought that supervision would simply melt away and that employees would no longer be accountable for their work. Some assumed they would not have to work so hard. Of course, it made no sense. Employee ownership doesn't change the need for hard work.

Employee ownership also had an important impact on business strategy at United, and one of the best examples was the opportunity a few years ago to buy US Airways. Secrecy has always been one of the most powerful tools, and sometimes one of the most powerful weapons, in corporate mergers. But that particular part of the arsenal can be awkward when a company's employees are also its owners.

The offer to buy came to me at the beginning of 1997, when the CEO of US Airways asked me whether United wanted to consider buying his company. After a short discussion with my senior management, we concluded the idea had real merit.

It made a lot of sense.

US Airways was strong on the East Coast and United was not. We decided that because we were employee-owned, we would have all of our discussions about this purchase in the open.

Typically, this kind of merger deal making happens behind closed doors. A handful of executives from both companies work quietly behind the scenes and have little to say publicly about the matter until a deal is struck.

We went a different direction in connection with the US Airways opportunity. First, we went public, and second, we made crystal clear the four tests we needed to pass before we were willing to make an offer to buy. And doing it in the open gave us the chance to keep tabs on what our own employees thought about the idea.

The tests were important, because we knew if we failed any of them, the idea was doomed. United and US Airways employees had to be willing to accept the merger on both sides; we didn't want to see a deferral of more than a year or so in achieving investment-grade credit ratings; we needed to believe the combined company would yield more profits for shareholders within a year or two; and US Airways employees would have to be employee owners, too, under a fair formula.

We failed an important one.

We were able to learn that both groups of employees—at United and US Airways—just weren't ready for a merger. US Airways employees were not convinced their company was in bad shape. They were not willing to make any of the sacrifices that would be required in a merger. And our employees were so focused on seniority rights that they didn't want to get involved in the difficulties they saw coming if we were to merge the United and US Airways seniority lists.

That situation is peculiar to airlines, where employees get more pay and privileges based on seniority. Pilots get to fly bigger airplanes and get paid more to do it. Mechanics get off the midnight shifts sooner.

Airline employees consider it unjust that, in a merger situation, some employees from another airline might be able to come in higher on the seniority system than they are. It would slow the pace of their own advancement.

We had not made enough progress to resolve United's own cultural questions. To merge those two companies given the strong feelings in the workforces would have added yet another culture challenge.

In the end, we did not go forward with the US Airways merger at that time primarily because of these employee issues. That was unfortunate because it would have been a smart business decision. Ironically, even with the merged seniority, our employees would have been better off because the combined company could have grown faster, and that would have accelerated pay opportunities and other seniority-related benefits faster for both United and US Airways employees.

At the time we were in discussions, US Airways stock was at about $12 a share. I imagine we could have bought it at $17 or $18 a share. As I write this chapter it is selling at $29 a share. And we are now in a competitive battle with US Airways, among others, in the east at Washington's Dulles International Airport.

(As this book was in preparation, the United purchase of US Airways was being revived.)

The plan has shifted to Washington now, and I think it could take quite some time for the U.S. Department of Justice to decide whether the merger should go through. The problems with labor negotiations and service interruptions over the summer are going to complicate that decision, but I still think it is a good business decision. The major difference this time around is that one of United's unions representing about half of all the employees would like this merger to happen.

United had plenty of regular business issues, of course, unrelated to people and culture. We all knew that, although we were the largest airline in the world, we couldn't fly to all the world's major cities. We would have had to triple in size to do that.

How do you triple in size without tripling in size?

For United, the answer was Star Alliance.

The goal was to promise our United customers that even if we didn't fly to a location, we could get them there with one seamless connection inside our alliance system of airlines. Frequent passengers on United get special upgrades and other rewards. We wanted those folks treated the same special way if they flew on the planes of our alliance partners.

As the King of Frequent Flyers, I know all about the miseries of long-distance air travel. Take, for example, my trip from Aspen to Katmandu.

I took United Express from Aspen to Denver, Denver to Chicago on United, United from Chicago to Narita, Japan, then Narita to Bangkok on Thai Airways, and Bangkok to Katmandu on Thai, which is, fortunately, one of United's Star Alliance partners.

Obviously, to make this kind of system work, we had to reciprocate for our alliance airline partners' customers. For us, it meant potential profits. In 1998, United achieved about $225 million in profits from all its alliances. In my opinion, the alliance can grow to produce some $500 million to $600 million in profits for United over time. There are now thirteen top-tier airlines around the world that form the Star Alliance and they are a couple of years ahead of the next best alliance in the industry. I am most proud that the alliance is built on trust and support, not primarily on hard-fought contracts or shared ownership.

I have had my share of disappointments at United, but I don't think anything quite compares to my experience in identifying a successor. I thought I had learned a clear lesson at Chrysler that would help me in setting the stage for my own successor at United. It is one of a CEO's most important responsibilities.

I believe the United board and I created America's best succession plan. It doesn't just happen at the top of the company. Planning needs to go anywhere from 40 to 150 people deep, depending on the size of the business. A CEO needs to develop the kind of people who are capable of running the company. I thought we had prepared for that, and my likely successor, my own CEO-in-waiting, was to be John Edwardson.

And we had plans from within to move people up behind him.

For reasons I don't get, a few of the union leaders thought John was not right for the job. The view down deep, I came to understand, was that he was not sympathetic to unions. In all of my years of working with John, I never saw that problem. But the perception was there from the beginning, and no one was able to change it.

Ever since I came to United, I tried very hard to take on the tough, difficult cases, the ones that brought the company face-to-face in conflict with its unions. For much of my last year on the job, I kept John away from those controversies.

I handled the midterm pay scrap. I handled the issue of regional jets, a hot topic with pilots at all the major airlines. The advent of smaller jets gives us all the chance to put jet service into the feeder regional airlines. United's pilots have a clause in their contract giving them the right to refuse those jets going into the feeder system. Those planes would be flown by pilots for the regional airlines who are not United union members. Their salaries are lower and their pay scales are different.

But handling those issues myself did not clear the way for John to rise to the CEO position.

It became clear some union leaders were digging in, and because of the way the company is structured, the unions carry a lot of weight.

Most unionized companies in America, incidentally, much prefer to choose leaders who get along with their unions. In our case, because of employee ownership, the union influence gets more media and Wall Street scrutiny.

In any case, I should have seen this coming. I should have seen it coming long ago and moved to solve the problem, but I didn't. Instead, I kept hoping the union folks would come around. I had spent all of these years talking about and thinking about company culture, but I failed to recognize what a strong role it played in the union.

I think John acted with great class. He decided to resign. I have no doubts about him or his future. He landed on his feet as CEO of Borg-Warner (now Burns International) and will be a great CEO.

We have now picked my successor, and I think he's another terrific choice. We went through our own painstaking procedure and searched all over the world. We took a hard look at Lou Hughes, the number three executive at General Motors. He was a great candidate and I believe America is going to hear a lot about him.

But the man who would get the job was always right here at United.

Jim Goodwin, fifty-three, is a thirty-two-year United veteran. We found over a five-month search that he was the template we were using to measure all of the other candidates who wanted the job.

That's a strong sign of what the board and what United think of him. Instead of trying to find someone who met the standard, we turned to the veteran who had become the standard. Then we filled in under Jim with twelve internal promotions, all strong candidates, a great confirmation of five years of succession and development planning at United.

Jim's roots run deep at United. He has experience in just about every part of the company, including its international division, which he ran. He understands and gets along with the unions.

I had a chance to test him with some outside groups, and he passed with flying colors. He spoke in my place at a conference in England. He addressed audiences on Wall Street and in Washington. He is passionate about United Airlines.

An inside story about him.

In thirty-two years on the job, he has never asked for a raise. He always figured he would just put his head down and get the job done.

We could have had both Edwardson and Goodwin, and United would have been even stronger for having them both in the company. It is an unusual feeling, the sadness at seeing a great candidate leave and the happiness at finding such a strong successor, all mixed up in one event.

Even this far into my career, I continue to learn.

I left United in a much stronger financial position than it was when I arrived, for its employees, for its shareholders, and for its customers, too. We went from number eight in profit margins to number three among all the world's major airlines. And at about $2.1 billion in 1998, we were number one in operating profit. That was quite a change in fortune. Before 1994, United's biggest annual operating profit had been $600 million.

We did it without layoffs. We grew in employment from 76,000 to 100,000 and we presented opportunities for all employees ready to take advantage of them. All the measures of employee performance were up. And all the signs of big trouble—absenteeism, grievances, workmen's compensation costs—were down.

It was a much better place to work.

But most important of all, United Airlines is a company to watch in this new century.

We may very well have created a standard for employee ownership and a company capable of satisfying customers in a superior way.

We weren't exactly at the top of that mountain when I walked out of my office for the last time, but we were a long way from the foothills I was looking at on the day I walked in.

A confession.

Some things move me to tears. Saving Chrysler did that to me. And so did leaving United.

On my last day at the office, I was called to a big barn of a room down in the basement of world headquarters. The people I work with, my fellow owners, had cleared the place out and turned it into a world communications center. They had contacted every significant United office around the world, and each office had responded with a banner, with posters, all of them carrying the signatures of the people I had worked with for five years.

Jim Goodwin said nice things. A lot of other people said nice things.

I got up to say nice things, but I cried a bit instead.

Just when I thought it was over, they put me on a high bar stool. Anybody who wanted to say goodbye was welcome to come up.

There were four hundred takers.

What stuck with me from that moment was that United had become a very different company. People were excited about it now.

Tears and all, the view from where I sat on the mountain was wonderful.

It didn't feel so comforting when United got into trouble a few months after I left. But I remain confident about the people who work there. I believe they will be diligent about getting back to focusing on the customer.

I would hope they have learned a lesson in the process. The employees have to understand that it is in their interest to resolve those disputes before they damage customer service, no matter how complicated the challenge might seem.

EIGHT

★

Dealing with Deep Trouble

Leaving United presented me with one of those rare business rewards, the sense that I had taken part in something that worked, and ultimately that worked very well.

But I can't sit smugly with that feeling without visiting the other side of the experience, that smack in the face you get when you realize something isn't working.

The sting goes right down into the gut and sets off all your alarms.

You get that fight-or-flight feeling.

I have to go back to my early Chrysler years to tell you how that feels.

I recall a Monday at Chrysler just after I arrived in 1979 in which I had no idea how we would meet the payroll, and that was one of my responsibilities as vice president and controller.

This problem loomed, a payday question mark that was hundreds of millions of dollars in size in a company that was already $1 billion in debt and floundering. It meant 140,000 anxious workers, already full of defeat and pessimism, might be pushed to the brink.

The perception of Chrysler was almost as bad as its problems.

I recall a meeting on April 1, 1980, with thirty-five bankers at Chrysler headquarters in New York. We were making some progress on financial questions, so we decided we would work right through lunch, sending out to a nearby deli for sandwiches.

We put our sandwich orders together and sent someone out to pick them up.

He came back a little while later and sheepishly announced he got a surprise when he asked them to send the bill to Chrysler.

"They said because it was Chrysler, they wanted the money up front," he reported.

How bad was Chrysler's problem?

If I knew how bad it was going to look the day I walked in the door, I would have been afraid to walk in the door.

Numbers simply don't convey the depth of the problem. We were headed toward the biggest single quarter operating loss in the history of American business.

The world's bankers would not lend Chrysler one more dime.

What I found at Chrysler, and how I responded to it, was one of my earliest lessons in dealing with a condition that is almost inevitable in cyclical business: how to handle hard times.

It might be a recession that comes along and deals a blow to your otherwise healthy company. Or you might find yourself in your own version of a Chrysler situation, arriving at a business that has been mismanaged to the point of death, a company already in deep decline and in need of desperate measures.

In any case, fixing that kind of damage is as much a question of mind-set as it is a question of finance or operations. You cannot think your way through bad times, but you cannot work your way through bad times without some advance thought.

You need a plan that fixes the problem at its heart.

At Chrysler, that meant an ardent and realistic pursuit of federal loan guarantees so we could get new, and more, money until we could restore the company to profits. It also meant a new relationship with our suppliers so they could understand that Chrysler's survival was so much in their interest that they should bend their rules to continue supplying parts even though we couldn't pay for a while. And it called for an aggressive assault on the marketplace to offer customers cars they actually wanted to buy.

It meant a new relationship with Chrysler's unions, too, because the company's survival would depend on its ability to shrink divisions it no longer needed and cut payroll costs among the workers who remained.

But all that would come later.

I had the dubious honor early in my Chrysler career of recording the biggest quarterly operating loss in U.S. business history. At the close of 1979, the figure was $250 million.

The worst-case scenario had come true.

One of the biggest companies in the United States was literally bleeding cash. We had gone from selling two million cars a year to selling one million cars a year.

It was clear we were making the wrong cars. And even the cars we made, we made the wrong way. Chrysler was still producing muscle cars, big V-8s, while the rest of the car industry was offering smaller and more efficient cars. I suspect the company viewed muscle cars as one of its legacies, those big fast Plymouths and Dodges.

They drank fuel and some of them were the size of ocean liners.

Add-ons were mother's milk of the car industry. Start with the basic car and then layer on the options. It was a great way to make profits and keep customers happy, too. But Chrysler was so far behind the times it was not even able to tell how much money it was making from the options it was putting on the cars. And that meant it didn't know what options to offer, what customers actually wanted, what actually sold.

Chrysler was all but finished, even though a few of us were determined to bring the company back to life. New on the job, I felt the enormous weight of Chrysler's problems had settled on me. I was the money man. The more I learned, the more I had to learn. And there was no time.

No one seemed to have any idea of where responsibility for all of these many problems actually rested at Chrysler. Everyone said costs must be controlled, but no one actually controlled them. The debt burden was crushing.

It didn't take me long to settle on the nature of the problem.

The top management people at Chrysler were not connected to the marketplace in any way that would tell them what consumers wanted, what they would buy, and what price they would pay. That was the message behind the steep decline in sales, but it was missed at headquarters.

They saw no need for a discipline I consider vital, making certain someone had primary responsibility for every element of revenue, every element of expense, and every element of the balance sheet, both in terms of assets and liabilities.

There were hundreds of creditors.

The big-city banks and financiers in Beirut and Tehran were waiting for money from Chrysler, along with bankers in Rockford, Illinois, and dozens and dozens of other small towns.

The company had already announced that only help from Washington would save Chrysler. That created even more panic among our lenders. They were canceling lines of credit left and right.

But it also revealed Chrysler's unrealistic view of itself, that as car company number three behind GM and Ford, it deserved some special consideration from the federal government.

At the same time, we were carrying whatever is below a junk bond credit rating and no more new money was available to us from anywhere on the planet.

The price tag for vehicle warranty work was costing Chrysler $300 million a year—the bill for shipping cars that had been poorly constructed—but no one seemed to know which problems we were repairing and what might be done to make the cars more dependable before they left the plants.

Chrysler management considered these quality problems as little more than an abstraction. They had all the data they needed to understand what was happening, why so many cars were coming off the line with defects, but they seemed to pay little or no attention to it.

In that atmosphere, the squeaking ashtray carries the same weight as an engine that mysteriously stops. In the real world, a customer cares a lot less about squeaks and a lot more about a car that just stops running, but Chrysler didn't understand that distinction.

It was sufficient at Chrysler to keep a list of what was going wrong. It made no effort I could discern to fix the problems.

My message from the Chrysler years is brief and quite direct: When things start going bad, always assume the worst, but try to project a clear message that you are not accepting the status quo, that you are fighting every day to bring your company back to life.

That's not to say you need to wear black armbands at work, scowl a lot, and treat people as if they were the crew on the *Titanic*.

Quite the contrary. Having faced reality and having devised a plan for changing it, you should be communicating two things to everyone. One is your confidence and the other is the substance of the plan.

In short, you have to show everyone that you believe all is not lost and they have to understand the basis of your confidence and to recognize that they have an important part in it.

But a CEO and his team can't get too scattered in sending that message. You must try to stay with the core elements of the plan and communicate them until you are literally sick of hearing about them.

At Chrysler, there were two core elements that we kept hammering into everyone. The first was that we would concentrate on cash flow to the exclusion of everything else until cash flow turned positive. The second was that we would be able to break even selling just one million cars a year.

The cash flow problem was obvious.

Under the old Chrysler formula, if you lost a dollar, you just went out and borrowed another dollar to replace it. That was no longer an option, so we had to transform the company's operations so that they were creating cash.

I ran into fantasy planning in my pursuit of this problem and that discovery cut straight to the heart of the question of car sales. There had been too many years and too many quarters of wishful thinking about how good Chrysler's cars were and how many cars the company could sell. People would build their plans on those assumptions and estimates.

The reality was simple: Chrysler could sell a million cars a year.

The fantasy projection went far beyond that number because planners needed to justify their expense requests on an assumption that car sales would increase.

The reality became apparent as quarterly sales simply did not meet those goals. Costs constantly exceeded the actual sales.

That is why it was so important to convince everyone that Chrysler had to break even despite the fact that it was selling only a million cars, half the number it had sold in healthier times.

There is another tool that is very important in hard times, but that must be tailored to the individual situation.

Never overlook the value of symbolism. I used to resist the idea, but I have come to embrace it over the years.

You need to tell your people that you are short of money

and that you have decided to unscrew every other light bulb in the company's headquarters. There will be resistance. People will want to know how much money that will save. But that is not the point. You want to send a message to everyone that hard times—dark times, too—have arrived.

We had a lovely old Art Deco headquarters for Chrysler. It had big, wide corridors and lovely offices for all of the executives on the top floor. But the carpeting was tattered and was long overdue for replacement. We didn't replace the carpet. We viewed it as a symbol. We wanted every employee and creditor who walked into the executive suite to notice it.

We made our symbolic mistakes, too.

Chrysler had an airplane, and Lee Iacocca made a bad decision one spring when his buddy George Steinbrenner invited him to Florida to watch the Yankees in spring training. There we were, arguing for our very lives in Washington, begging, and the boss gets his picture in the paper with Steinbrenner at spring training, having flown on the company plane!

You don't have to wear tattered suits and shoes with holes in the bottom, but in hard times, it doesn't hurt to look a little frayed around the edges.

Troubles so deep change the realities at work at the top of a company.

You must learn how to negotiate from weakness, to turn your creditors into allies and your suppliers into partners by helping them recognize that your survival and their best interests are very much the same subject.

Keep giving me parts and I will build good cars and sell them and pay you later, under a schedule that represents fairness to everyone standing in line. Make it a promise and live up to it.

And don't be afraid to take daring steps.

Get a good bankruptcy attorney on board, for example.

I am not suggesting bankruptcy is the best solution. That is not why you want this specialist at your side. His or her job will be to help you persuade bankers and suppliers to help, establish some priorities, and provide some different perspectives on how to handle the problem.

I learned that lesson in my first year at Chrysler, when the financial problems were so deep that bankruptcy was a possibility.

Don Riegle was one of Michigan's U.S. senators when we were working hard in Washington to get help. He called me one afternoon and suggested I talk to an attorney he knew, Ron Trost, who specialized in bankruptcy.

Trost suggested that all of our creditors were looking at Chrysler as though it were two entities, the factories company that made the cars and the finance company that helped finance the cars for dealers. The factories were in debt to the tune of $1 billion and the finance company had debts of $3 billion.

No one realized it at the time, but the banks weren't very worried whether we could save the car-making factory part of the business with $1 billion in debts because they assumed they could still tap the finance company to get their $3 billion if the factories closed.

I asked the attorney to work with Steve Miller on the Chrysler staff to come up with a solution, which we would present at a big meeting of our bankers. A couple of days later, off we went to New York. The bankruptcy attorney went through his speech, explaining the realities to the bankers.

He told them they would not have first claim on the finance company assets if the factories closed. The first claimant would be the federal government, because, under federal law, it would be able to grab those assets to cover the pension costs of the Chrysler factory workers who would lose their jobs if the factories closed.

The bankers were shocked.

They called us names. We were sons of bitches for hiding this from them, they said. They thought we had known this all along and that we were just being clever or devious. They really didn't want to admit that they had never thought of the pension liability problem themselves.

It was human nature at its worst, bankers looking for some place to shift the blame for not doing their own homework.

It took about a day for the situation to calm down.

Quickly, the creditors recognized exactly what we recognized. Looking at Chrysler as a collapsing manufacturer with a big pot of money available at its finance company was wrong. Their best interests would be served in helping us keep the carmaker alive.

I know hiring a bankruptcy attorney sounds spooky.

It sounds like bringing the Angel of Death in, doesn't it? It's not the kind of decision you announce in a news release. You want to be quiet about seeking this kind of help. But that doesn't mean it is not valuable.

Bankruptcy is a specialty.

A good attorney will be able to tell you quickly whether you need to get into Chapter 11, and he will also advise you that you have to go into that position with some cash on hand. There is not much a judge can do to help a company that has no cash.

If you wait until the last dime is gone, Chapter 11 will almost certainly lead to Chapter 7, which is liquidation.

A really good CEO is a chameleon.

Sometimes that means he has to be a bastard, even though the role doesn't seem to fit. Sometimes he can be a nice guy, a strong leader who builds consensus among his employees. All of the time, he has to know which role to play, and, just like a chameleon, he has to be able to change his colors if that is necessary.

I was tough in those early Chrysler years, and I trained the people who worked under me to be tough. It wasn't hard, even though their natural instincts were not to be tough. They knew it was necessary. A lot of people who had thought of working at Chrysler as a lifetime meal ticket faced the possibility of losing their jobs. There were layoffs and cutbacks almost everywhere. But it wasn't as though we had an option. We were not being ruthless because we liked that kind of behavior. Chrysler's survival called for it.

I was fortunate in that I had terrific people who were with me at the time: Jerry York, who became vice chairman of Chrysler and later CFO of IBM, Fred Zuckerman, Chrysler's treasurer and later treasurer of RJR Nabisco and IBM, and Steve Miller, who became vice chairman at Chrysler.

It took me a few weeks after my arrival to start identifying another class of Chrysler characters who would become invaluable. Call them the truth tellers. Tom Pappert was in charge of sales. I could always call him and ask for the real numbers, despite the company's fantasy planning penchant. The chief engineer and the fleet manager were just as reliable. Within sixty days, I knew who to go to, and I was right nine out of ten times. Within two years, I was right ten out of ten times.

I started out thinking I would trust everyone individually until they had lost that trust. That was not a safe approach, but I had no other choice. My goal was to identify the people I could trust, then ask them who they trusted, then use those names to build my own truth-telling network inside Chrysler.

I don't remember eating much, sleeping much, or spending much time at all with my family during that crisis. It was all about work all of the time. But that was what it took, first, to stop the bleeding, nurse the patient back to health, and finally get it back on its feet again.

One of Chrysler's big problems was that it was trying to handle the challenge virtually alone. Even by 1979, it was clear to me that no one could deliver a successful turnaround without cleaning house and bringing in new people.

I reached out.

Salomon Brothers sent a team of ten headed by senior partner James Wolfensohn, later head of the World Bank. We also had access to a vast collection of banking community lawyers who were deeply experienced in dealing with large, troubled creditors.

You learn a lot about bankers when your company is in trouble.

The most important lesson is that you must treat them so evenhandedly that no one has a complaint. The worst thing in the world is for one banker to find out you are treating another banker better.

There is one important sign to watch for that tells you that you don't know how much trouble you are really in. The friendly banker, the one who wanted to build his portfolio and who offered fantastic rates and good lunches and lots of affirmation, calls up and says he would like to introduce you to one of his special colleagues.

That colleague is from the work-out department, which is responsible for collecting bad loans. He may want to take you to lunch, too. The difference is that you will be the main item on the menu.

When that day comes, you had better start reacting and fast, because those are the people who come to clean up after the party. I have never figured out whether banks deliberately pick mean, tough people for those jobs, or whether those jobs turn them into mean, tough people.

It is a distinction without a difference.

Sometimes, these hard realities change the way you think about finance. For me, for example, letters of credit had always been one area in which no flexibility was allowed. You paid them no matter what.

But we had a problem at Chrysler. We had a special relationship with Mitsubishi in Japan. We were buying their cars on letters of credit, and paying on those letters even in

our darkest days. Our other creditors thought that was unfair, and that led me to make an unprecedented decision.
I asked the Japanese to wait, too. They didn't like it, but
they went along with the plan.

We got solid advice from President Carter's Treasury Department, fresh from its experience in helping bail out
New York City.

Treasury told us we simply could not do the job with just
the team we had in place.

I headed a core group of five or six officers when I arrived at Chrysler. Treasury suggested I become the chief of
a task force of thirty to forty people, each of whom would
be assigned a specific task in the turnaround.

I brought in Steve Miller from my days at Ford in
Venezuela.

Then I reached deep down into Chrysler and began a
search for the thirty- to forty-year-old executives who were
full of energy and ideas, but stuck under a bushel basket in
such a confused, traditional corporation. I had to get rid of
some people, too, which I didn't enjoy. But short-term
kindness seldom pays off in the long run, particularly when
you are responsible for a business that is in such deep trouble.

I took a close, early look at operations.

Accounts payable was just one of the nightmares I
found. This is a crucial function for a company facing daily
cash pressures, but Chrysler had it spread over thirty different locations. I moved quickly to centralize that function.

I started the same process in purchasing, payroll, and facilities forecasting. We no longer wanted to have those
functions spread all over the company.

I even attacked daily procedures. Chrysler could no
longer operate as though it were going to last forever. I
knew in 1979 the question was whether this company could
last even a few more weeks. It would do me no good to wait

five weeks to learn that a cash crisis had developed some-where in such a huge company.

We shifted into a crisis mode and started shedding bu-reaucratic procedures left and right. That was aimed at forcing our cash shortages to surface instantly.

An amazing clarity develops among all the participants when a company is that close to disaster. There is a sense of common purpose. It cuts across the divisions and imagi-nary lines that separate people in better times. Unions, I found at Chrysler, are ready to talk and deal once they re-alize the nature of a company's problem.

This clarity reaches beyond your own payroll and out into the businesses and people the company touches. Al-most everyone is willing to cooperate if they recognize that the pain is being shared fairly and evenly, and that the profits will be shared, too, if the company is revived. It is a question of fairness, and it doesn't stop with bankers.

It stretches across your company, from the executive suites down to the little room in the basement where the cleaning people collect their mops and soap so everything can be scrubbed up overnight. And it reaches beyond your own turf and into the corporate suites of your suppliers and customers.

Think of all of these people, from the banks to the sup-pliers to the employees, as constituents who are involved ei-ther in your failure or your success. That was the basic message the bankruptcy attorney delivered to Chrysler's banks. If everyone believes they are being treated fairly, you can move mountains.

I call it equality of sacrifice.

It is a philosophy developed at Chrysler and I have es-poused it ever since. During the administration of Presi-dent Ronald Reagan, when the federal deficit was so high, I even advanced an equality of sacrifice project for the fed-eral government.

It got completely tangled up in the political debate that

pitted defense spending against social spending and went
nowhere. As a result, it took years to finally address the
federal budget deficit problem.

At Chrysler, equality of sacrifice meant you had to look
at every person, every entity that had a stake in Chrysler's
survival, and you had to create a form of equal sacrifice or
risk. You had to make that very clear to the company's constituents.

We would be asking taxpayers to face the prospect that
if Chrysler failed, the federal government would have to
make good on $1.5 billion in loan guarantees. In five states
where Chrysler had significant numbers of workers, with
the federal government of Canada and the provincial government of Ontario, we sent the same message. Everyone
needed to find a way to lend Chrysler some money, which
taxpayers would lose if Chrysler failed.

Suppliers had to keep producing for a while without getting paid. They bought a form of preferred stock, which we
called supplier-preferred stock, that would give them a
share in the company's eventual success.

Chrysler's employees had to sacrifice, too. Some got laid
off, which was the ultimate sacrifice, and all took pay concessions. Lee Iacocca took his first year's salary in stock.
The officers all accepted 10 percent pay cuts.

Iacocca's gesture was crucial.

These days you might think, "What's the big deal? He
got paid in stock."

But to understand the brilliance of the move, you have
to realize that no one wanted Chrysler stock when Iacocca
made that announcement. Almost everyone thought
Chrysler was going under and they would end up with wallpaper if they chose stock over salary.

Iacocca's decision to take virtually no pay embarrassed
all the officers into accepting that 10 percent salary cut. It
was a message to everyone that the people who were per-
ceived as fat cats would be sacrificing first, and that opened

the doorway to sacrifice, and ultimately success, all over the company.

It wasn't easy but it helped when those at the top of the company sacrificed first. If you have a large contingent of union members, you will find it very difficult to convince them to accept pay cuts, even though it helps if management goes first. Even Doug Fraser, who headed the United Auto Workers at the time and who still stands as one of the most intelligent and progressive union leaders of the era, thought it was a long shot to negotiate and ratify a contract that involved pay concessions.

But that was before Iacocca held a meeting with all the union workers. Everyone knew about his own pay cut.

He created a very dramatic moment.

"Look," he said, "I have lots of $17 an hour jobs. I have no $20 an hour jobs."

And that was the difference. Concessions were approved, but at the first opportunity, the first quarter of real profits, that mood changed and the union said it wanted full pay restored and got it.

Not true during the worst of times at Chrysler, but unions frequently refuse to do much of anything in pay concessions to help a company solve its problem.

Companies facing that kind of resistance often turn to cuts among their salaried employees. Based on my Chrysler experiences, I think cutting the pay of salaried employees only encourages them to move toward becoming union members themselves. That is not bad in itself, but during hard times it is counterproductive and creates an unfair, unbalanced, and demoralizing environment.

Equality of sacrifice isn't the kind of tool a CEO can use in flush times just to save on operating costs. What made it work at Chrysler was the awareness that the company was dying, and that desperate measures were needed.

Navigating the marketplace is like swimming with sharks. If you focus on one, you may feel safe, but in the interest of improving your chances of avoiding a serious problem, I strongly recommend using your peripheral vision.

At Chrysler, we had an economics staff of one.

That doesn't sound like much, considering that General Motors had three hundred. But it was more than sufficient because his contribution was to help the company develop its own set of indicators that were not only reasonably accurate, but predictive, sometimes out to twelve months. The tailored indicators covered many of the variables in the world of auto companies. Oil prices were crucial, for obvious reasons, as was the price of steel. The price of money played a central role all across the formula, not only for cash-strapped Chrysler but for all the people at all levels who were borrowing money to buy cars. General economic indicators played a role, too. If consumer confidence was weakening, we knew that would be playing out in the dealerships.

These were our own measures that were constructed from the experience of the company. We weren't passive about them at all.

We used them to craft what we called our red light, yellow light, and green light system. Every month, Don Hilty, our economist (quiet, determined, a veteran of the oil industry), would come to the board and tell us what to expect based on our own set of indicators. Each one of them had a red, yellow, or green light attached.

If we started seeing too many yellow lights, certainly some red lights, we knew it was time for Chrysler to move. If we saw nothing but green lights, we moved, too, because our own economic indicators were pointing the way to action.

This system helped us predict recessions and upturns before they came along. As important, it fit in with our own long-term plans for recovery. We certainly didn't want to go any deeper into debt and we wanted to end the kinds of practices that had been so damaging to Chrysler.

In 1988 and 1989, we found that too many of our measures started showing up yellow or red. We were very worried about consumer confidence and a federal measure the Carter administration had devised called "the misery index," which is all about how people think they are doing across a number of economic categories.

When we saw slippage in those two areas, we used that information to cut back on our spending and to forecast fewer car sales.

Those changes gave us a one-year advantage over our competitors when the market finally softened. They had to scramble, but we were prepared. We had time to plan.

The common wisdom says "Don't go looking for trouble."

Whoever said that wasn't a business executive, or for that matter, a leader of any kind. A good part of the job involves looking for trouble in order to detect the earliest possible warning signs of a problem. Often, that requires making some intuitive, seat-of-the-pants judgments, but that's why you sit in the big chair.

The willingness to go after problems and find indicators you trust are the most valuable qualities you can have in developing the mind-set you need to manage in hard times.

If my strongest piece of advice is "assume the worst," then just behind it is a simple piece of advice: "Don't just study, act."

Don't misunderstand me.

I am a great believer in the value of research and objective, comprehensive analysis. But your people can study your company deep into a recession when you should be taking remedial action. It does little good to have one of those "Eureka!" moments during which everyone recognizes that a recession has arrived.

You can't afford to make terrible mistakes in this process, but you can afford to make some less than terrible mistakes.

If you are right on eight out of ten actions, then you can go back later and fix the two you were wrong about. Having made those eight right decisions, you will be more than prepared to deal with the decline before an avalanche arrives and it is too late.

I made my own less than terrible mistake.

I pushed a plan that would have cut back on pension eligibility in the early 1980s. Iacocca was reluctant. I said we had to take very tough medicine to address our costs problem. As it turned out, I was wrong. The savings from the pension cutbacks amounted to about 5 percent of our cost-reduction program, but they caused turmoil all over the company.

We decided to back off, correcting a less than terrible mistake before it did too much damage.

I helped correct one of Chrysler's own less than terrible mistakes in 1984. I had concluded at about that time that Chrysler's prospects were so good that we didn't have to borrow any more money.

At about the same time, Iacocca had scheduled a meeting with me and the treasurer to move forward on a $600 million loan. The legal and treasury departments were very excited about having put this deal together.

The meeting began. Somewhat meekly, I said, "I don't think we have to borrow this money." It was as though I was not in the room. No one heard me. They kept on talking about how to close the loan. After all, we were just a year away from there being no one willing to lend to Chrysler.

I raised my decibel level: "I don't think we need the money."

Same response. I had no impact on the discussion.

Finally, I really screamed at them. It sounded as though I had sat on a pin.

"WE DON'T NEED THE MONEY!"

That got their attention. I suggested we drag our feet for thirty days, because by that time, we would see money pouring in from sales and savings in operations.

I had been heard and a less than terrible mistake was fixed.

As soon as you know that you have successfully addressed your cash flow problems during hard times, you must turn immediately to quality. Profits and the balance sheet and the shareholders can wait a little longer. You must immediately address the question of quality in the product or service you are producing and delivering.

It seems reasonable, doesn't it? But it is amazing how difficult it is for someone at the top of a company to recognize the real problem. The institution itself might be trying to hide that reality. Ego can get in the way, too, particularly for founders and entrepreneurs who have followed their own visions, instincts, and passions in building their companies.

I saw one of these ego-driven situations developing right in front of me at United, and it carried me back to my Chrysler days.

I don't think it would be fair to name the company, because our relationship has been terminated. But the example of what can happen is valuable because it shows so clearly how problems develop, how they don't get solved, and what the likely solutions might be.

We were not at all happy with the quality we were getting from one of our suppliers. We warned the supplier that we would cut back on the relationship unless quality improved.

The supplier had an interesting response. He told us that if United gave him higher prices, he would invest it in quality issues and solve our problem. I had my suspicions about that proposal, but I didn't want to close the door on the relationship too quickly. I had to find out what was really going on.

That was so much like what I had seen at Chrysler, I couldn't believe it. Former top Chrysler management simply could not admit that they were the cause of the company's problems. They had to blame anybody and everybody else, from customers to lenders to suppliers, even to the federal government.

I went to our United people for an assessment of how this company was doing, how well it was controlling its costs, how well it was taking care of its own business. I was open to the suggestion of higher prices. Sometimes that can solve the problem. But I didn't want to make that investment if the cash was going to be pumped into an inefficient business and ultimately down a rat hole.

The reports were not good.

This supplier didn't know its own costs and had mixed that problem in with a lot of other troubles, classic unintentional imitation of the Chrysler problem, to my way of thinking.

My sense was that the situation was about to get mean, but before we started cutting the relationship, I wanted to talk with the CEO to measure his perspective and hear what he had to say about the problem.

After listening to him, I gave him my own summary.

"Let me tell you what I am hearing," I said.

"I am hearing that there aren't any other needs, there aren't any other problems, and that it is really not a question of quality. You are saying it is not really a cost problem, either. The problem, as you see it, is that United simply isn't doing enough and that is all there is to it. The way you see it, there aren't any faults on your side."

Then I created a hypothetical situation, based on my own experience working with companies in trouble. I told him his biggest challenge would be to decide whether he could be objective in solving the problems of his own company. The implication was clear. He was unable to detach himself emotionally from what was all around him. He was not able to blame himself for anything, just as Chrysler management had been unable to recognize its own role in the decline of the company.

I told him that only he could decide if that was the case.

He was simply too close, too tied up in what he had created.

"Go hire somebody you really trust and put him or her in charge of your day-to-day operations. If you have the courage, go on vacation. If you don't have the courage to take a long vacation, then have the wisdom to stay out of his hair. Give him advice, but let him call the shots. You are bleeding cash. You are going to go into bankruptcy soon. Concentrate on getting your cash flow up. For God's sake, don't expand. Quit worrying about market share. Shrink some if you need to. Don't buy new assets for a while. Go look at your costs and find and look at every one of your expenses and see where you can really cut back."

He listened.

He was polite.

But he was also very tense. He never said he would or would not take the advice. About a week later I found out that he had made a major new investment in assets. He thought he was going to grow his way out of his problems. Shortly after the session, he left active employment, with the consent of his board, though he was a major shareholder.

I believe he made a typical mistake.

He had a great idea and a special talent. He was somewhat charismatic, and for years his sales figures kept climbing every month. His own family and his own community thought he was terrific. But he wasn't paying attention to his own costs and he didn't pay enough attention to the quality he was delivering to his customers. The day came when his sales growth stopped and it all came apart on him.

Much the same as with the people who ran Chrysler, he didn't understand the problem and he certainly didn't have the objectivity he needed to fix it. Had he been objective, had he designed his own set of accurate forecast measures to show how his company was doing, he might have avoided all that trouble in the first place.

He had an ego problem, and that is common when companies find themselves in trouble. Sometimes, the people in charge are so compelled by their own vision, their own experience, that they can't see the problem.

To my mind, that puts him into what I would define as the Three Categories of Captains of Industry in Hard Times.

First, there are the Founders.

It was literally their baby, their idea. They brought it to life and watched it thrive. But when trouble arrives, they really can't get past the belief that all problems are caused by someone else.

Second, there are the Managers.

They were there and maybe even created the mess, but they have a terrible time concentrating on the problem and its potential solutions. They have to spend most of their time justifying their actions and demonstrating that it wasn't their fault.

Third would be the Paratroopers.

These are the people who are dropped into a company. They have no previous baggage, but they know the industry and they can be objective. They just roll up their sleeves and go at it.

I am not saying the paratroopers are the only answer to deep business problems, but the odds of success increase as one moves through these three categories. Category three means fresh air and fresh eyes to assess the problem. There is no interest in hiding from responsibility or fixing blame elsewhere.

Remember that this advice is coming from a veteran paratrooper.

There is one other element to factor into the formula for management in bad times that is just impossible to measure.

In bad times, you need some good luck.

Sometimes, you can create a little of your own. And

sometimes, it just seems as though someone up there is watching and has decided for his own reasons that it is time to sprinkle a little good luck your way.

We were within hours of running out of money at Chrysler in June 1980.

We had obtained everything we needed to take advantage of those loan guarantees from the federal government the instant the agreements were signed. All we had to do was sign for Chrysler at a formal settlement meeting at a law firm in New York.

I had flown into Manhattan from Detroit. I was to sign for the company. Time was running out. I was just about to the door of the Westvāco building in New York, where one of the law firms was located, when my driver runs into a whole fleet of fire trucks. The street was full of hoses. I told the driver I would just walk the last few steps. I went about ten feet and who do I run into but Steve Miller and a bunch of other Chrysler guys and advisers. They are looking up into the sky.

The twentieth floor of the Westvāco building is on fire.

All of the documents we need to save Chrysler, about a million of them, are up there on the thirty-second floor, neatly laid out on the table awaiting my signature. They look at me and I am getting nervous.

If those papers burn, Chrysler is going down.

We did the only thing we could do. We went to dinner to talk about it. One of the New York people appears at the restaurant. He notes that if they contain the fire, everything could be okay, but that if the owner finds out about it, he won't let us in the building right away because of his insurance liabilities. Even if the papers survived the fire, everything would be lost.

We were all but out of money.

We concluded we had to get to the owner before anyone else did.

Meanwhile, huge panes of glass are bursting out of the building and crashing onto 49th Street at Park Avenue. Big orange flames are exploding from the twentieth floor. Now I was beyond being nervous. The fire department and the owner said wait awhile until it cools down, then you can go in.

My people said I was just too nervous to deal with it, so they sent me back to my hotel to sleep, as if I could. They went to all-night grocery stores and borrowed shopping carts. Then they walked up into the still-smoldering, hot building and loaded the million documents into grocery carts and hauled them along Lexington Avenue to another law firm in the Citicorp building.

What a night!

At 3:00 A.M., they called me and said, "Come and sign."

To this day, if you look at the documents that saved Chrysler, they carry an elegant gray border.

That's smoke damage.

While good luck helps, management in hard times requires quick thinking and quick action. But it is always better to come up with a plan before the trouble actually arrives.

Even though it might seem as though everything is going up in flames, keep an eye open for good luck.

Think of ways to create some of your own. If shopping carts are what you need to make it all work out in the middle of the night, don't be shy about asking for them.

NINE

★

Two Forbidden Words: Trust Me

I have a memory of a very young man standing in a stairwell in a dress factory in St. Louis back in the 1950s.

Those were hard times for the people who worked sewing clothing. The companies were tough and were fighting to keep organized labor out.

It had always been a low-wage business that was constructed on an endless supply of immigrants and poor people who were so desperate for work that they were willing to suffer all kinds of abuses just to keep bread and a little meat on the table for their families.

At the same time, the workers should have known their best course of action was to unionize and negotiate for improvements.

The battle between the people who owned companies and the people who worked for them had been under way for decades by that time. Unions were growing stronger, leaving a legacy of good contracts, better wages and benefits, and a body of labor law that would change the nature of the relationship between capital and workers in the United States.

It was a romantic quest in many ways.

I know all about it because I was the young man standing in the stairwell.

It seems like a long time ago now, but the memories come racing back to me after so many years in manage-

ment at Ford, Chrysler, and United Airlines. I suppose I
was always viewed as a boss, someone to mistrust, by many
of the union leaders and members I worked with over the
years.

I wish I could have found some way to take them back in
time with me, to show them where I came from. It might
have changed their attitude about me, and it might have
showed them that in many cases their interests and my interests were the same.

The International Ladies' Garment Workers' Union was
struggling to win representation at that St. Louis factory.
Every day, the workers would come down the steps and
walk out the front gate. People who worked those kinds of
jobs just loved the end of the day. They didn't drag themselves out of the factory, they rushed out, eager to get to
the comfort of their families and the pleasures of the dinner table.

Or at the very least, off to get a drink.

My job was simple.

I had to slow everyone down so some other union folks
could approach them and ask them to sign cards that
would clear the way for a union election. The company's
job in those days was to do whatever it could to get me out
of that stairwell.

I was a kid on summer break from Princeton. Organized
labor had become my passion. I had studied the histories
of the great labor movements and the development of
labor philosophy.

My senior thesis at Princeton was an examination of a
long strike between the electrical workers union and West-
inghouse, an assignment that gave me access to everyone
from corporate people to union leaders to mediators who
worked on settling the strike. That was one of the great advantages of having a Princeton professor who was also a
federal mediator.

Looking closely at that strike, I concluded that it might
have been avoided if there had been better communica-

tion on all sides. The U.S. Senate got involved, too, and conducted hearings that did nothing but make the situation worse. I believed labor and management could have solved their problems much more quickly without meddling from Congress.

I was trying to decide what I would do with this terrific education I had at Princeton and the union movement was presenting an opportunity.

I ended up going into management with Ford Motor Co., but at that stage, I could have gone either way, because I knew what I wanted was a job in labor relations.

Even at that age, I had a good start on understanding what organized labor was all about. Why Ford? In those days, and probably in these days, too, organized labor never sent recruiters to campus to look for new prospects.

Ford was the first in the door, and I took the offer.

I don't want to cry poor, but I did not come from money. I came from a Jewish immigrant family that paid its way selling chickens in St. Louis. We weren't that far removed from the old country, with its pogroms and its problems. I knew what it was like to live in a family where money was very tight.

I got to Princeton because I was an athlete and I had worked hard and had good grades. I did not live a life of comfort there. I waited my share of tables and scraped around for clothes and spending money.

By nature, then, my sentiments were not in the management camp, even though that is where I landed.

That is why I was there with the ILGWU, standing where I was certainly not at all welcome, trying to slow people down so they could hear why they should join the union.

I loved that job.

Even as a young college kid, I felt it made me a part of something much bigger, a little cog in the history of organized labor. I was Jerry Greenwald on the outside, with a little Walter Reuther close to the heart.

I didn't get to stand in the stairwell for long.

When the local union boss who had helped me get the job heard what I was actually doing, he told his team, "You can't make this kid do this, you're going to kill him!" He fired me after three weeks. He said I just wasn't cut out for that kind of work.

But I was having a good time. I never felt I was in physical danger. I don't think the union boss really cared about how well I was doing the job, he just didn't want me to get hurt because it would have been hard to explain why a Princeton college kid got busted up in a labor scrap at a dress factory.

Leaving that job didn't end my interest in unions and their history at all. It only whetted my appetite. My father had been a Roosevelt Democrat and was always concerned about the plight of the working people.

Reuther, who founded the United Auto Workers, was my hero.

I just couldn't put down the books that covered labor history.

It's still with me today, even after all these years in management. I wanted to help the dress factory workers in the mid-1950s, to be part of that cause, just as I wanted to help United Airlines workers when I joined the company to help with employee ownership.

The problem is that we are living in a different era now, one that has carried us far from the experiences and the conditions that were so central to the cause of unionization at mid-century. But the attitudes that played such a powerful role in that old struggle, demonizing management being one of the strongest, are still with us.

I was sitting at my desk at United a few months before my retirement thinking hard about that problem, which has its roots somewhere in the late nineteenth century. We are in a new century now, but we can't seem to shake the attitudes that were so powerful midway through the last one.

In Europe during the last half of the nineteenth century, workers identified ownership with aristocracy; in the U.S. it was identified with the robber baron entrepreneurs. In the twentieth century, that aristocracy faded because of heavy taxation. Major industries ceased to be run by the founding titans and their families, and public ownership became commonplace.

Organized labor needed a new villain, a tangible enemy: management. In most cases, management obliged by earning labor's enmity, particularly during the Great Depression, when those fortunate enough to have jobs felt extremely insecure.

The pessimism of respected figures hardly inspired confidence.

When the world's best known economist, John Maynard Keynes, was asked during the Great Depression if there had ever been such a time in human history, he answered, "Yes, it was called the Dark Ages."

World War II ended the Depression and the second half of the twentieth century has seen a surprising turn. Union membership has fallen to half of its high level. Industry has become global and the U.S. economy has gone from being driven by manufacturing to being powered by services—travel and tourism, banking and finance, retailing and technology.

But labor leaders and many managers have been slow to cope with that reality. Some of them have tried to keep alive the old militancy, but it no longer seems to fit, at least not here in the United States.

A few have begun to recognize that times have changed and that their future relies on developing a more cooperative relationship between labor and management.

I believe it is time now to reconstruct the relationship between management and labor to prepare for the challenges we face. My sense, based on the experiences I have collected over the past four decades, is that the most important part of that mission must center on the question of trust.

It is remarkable that attitudes that were born in the first part of the twentieth century still play such a determining role in what we try to achieve today, but the weight of history is undeniable.

We saw those old attitudes playing out at United last summer. It was clear to me once again that after all these years, the issue of trust still nags and aggravates.

It makes you take a deep breath.

It is astonishing that a management and a union with highly educated members (and at United, with both sides holding ownership in the company) would have to hurt their customers to solve their labor problems.

This was a strong message about the lingering issue of mistrust. It's time we all get over it. Still, it persists.

The people who ran companies a century ago were depicted as robber barons and the people who worked for them were cast as noble, hardworking, and decent victims of brutal capitalism. That was labor's version of the story.

On the management side, labor was viewed as potentially socialist, unrealistic, and determined to get whatever it could, whenever it could.

Sometimes unions were willing to wreck a company just to make their point. Owners and corporate officers viewed organized labor as a vast collection of threatening thugs who were determined, for their own reason, to ruin what was working very well for management.

A hundred years have passed, but bitterness and distrust are the legacies of that struggle.

And that is the problem I was thinking so hard about during my final months at United.

Labor still distrusts management. Management still distrusts labor.

The biggest problem with those attitudes is that just about everything else in the labor-management formula has changed. I know that after a long career in management, I certainly don't view labor with hostility. I marvel at the achievements of modern American workers. They are smarter, more ethical, more productive, and more engaging than at any point in the nation's history.

And everywhere from Ford to Chrysler to United, I have seen what can happen when that old gap between the people who run companies and the people who work for them begins to disappear. Smart people recognize the value of identifying common interests and goals, and believe me, there are a lot of smart people on both sides of the equation.

Bridging that gap, then, is one of the most important items on the agenda for the future. From my perspective and experience, trust is the steel you use to build that bridge.

We are embarking on a new century, with all of its problems and all of its challenges and all of its opportunities. But this cliché from distant history still haunts and threatens us.

Even at United Airlines, certainly one of the strongest examples at the end of the twentieth century of employee ownership, we have still failed to find a way to build the level of trust we need between labor and management. The employees own most of this company. I worked for them. I worked for the shareholders.

But I still faced unions who viewed me with suspicion, maybe sometimes even as an enemy. I still faced some union officials and employees who thought I was out to win some financial advantage for the company at their expense. I still faced an assumption that somewhere behind the curtains, there was the modern version of one of those old robber barons.

It remains, then, a question of trust.

Think about that word because it will be one of the most important elements in achieving success in the coming century. At some point, everyone must realize that the world of work has changed. This is a transformation that touches every part of a business.

Workers are not mindless automatons putting parts in

place on production lines. Instead, they are decision makers who play a direct role in the success of a business. This is particularly true of industries like airlines that provide direct services to their customers.

At any time on any day of the week, the United employee at the ticket counter carries a version of the responsibility I carried as a chief executive. Our roles are certainly different, but at the end of the day, if the customer is not satisfied, everyone at United suffers.

Look at it this way. The ultimate responsibility of a chief executive officer is to the customer, to satisfy the customer and make a profit while doing it. As an employee, the United Airlines customer service representative at the ticket counter is responsible for satisfying the customer and doing it as efficiently as possible.

That is where we coalesce.

I know that, and most of United's employees know that, too.

We are bound to one another by this business reality.

That is the message of ownership in the modern era, and it should transcend the labor-management history that sometimes causes such problems. Business is no longer about keeping capital from labor or fostering an atmosphere that separates everyone. It is about pulling everyone together and working toward commonly recognized goals.

I have had the good fortune to work with benevolent despots, with visionaries, with dreamers, and with fools.

I have seen bad management at work.

I remember my mission for Ford in Brazil in the mid-1960s, where I scouted out the Willys company and later went to serve as controller after it had been purchased by Ford.

Willys's Brazilian headquarters was run by a business despot of the first order. His bosses simply didn't ask him enough questions, and he ran the place as though it belonged to him, which it did not.

He literally rode in his limo all the way to his office.

He had an elevator installed in headquarters that would

deliver him, in his car, to his executive office on the eighth floor. He just got out of the back seat, walked a few steps, and was behind his desk.

I didn't realize the depths of his despotic behavior until I reviewed the annual bonus list and found the office coffee girl among those who were well compensated at bonus time.

One look at her and I knew exactly what was going on.

I think General Motors was despotic in the mid-1950s and 1960s, too. They were doing so well that their executives assumed they must be wonderful. They just couldn't believe they could do anything wrong.

When they introduced the Corvair into the market, and Ralph Nader started questioning the car's safety record, they immediately concluded there must be something wrong with Ralph Nader, but not the car.

Contact with visionaries offset that experience, and I think one of the strongest of the lot was Doug Fraser of the United Auto Workers. He saw the importance of unions dealing with social injustice, and he found ways to cooperate with management to advance the interests of workers.

Carol Shelby was a visionary and a dreamer, too. Here is this country boy in bib and tucker overalls from a chicken farm in East Texas who dreamed he was going to be the first American to win Le Mans, and by God, he was. And then he wanted to build the first American car to win that race, the Ford Cobra, and he did that, too.

And what greater visionary was there than Lee Iacocca, first at Ford and then at Chrysler. He had a dream about a world auto company, the best of America, Japan, and Europe. Sounds like Daimler-Benz, doesn't it? Except he wanted the headquarters in Detroit.

Then there were the fools.

I remember the man who headed Richier, the French company I went to run after it was purchased by Ford. He was convinced he was going to be a Ford man, but that he was going to continue running Richier the French way. About two weeks after I arrived, I knew it wasn't going to work. I suspected Ford would eat him alive by insisting he do everything the Ford way, which is exactly what happened.

I have bought a lot of companies from their founders over the years, and I ran into some fools there, too. I have yet to see any of them happy that they sold their companies. They fell into the same trap. They were fools because they didn't have confidence in their own companies. They needed someone from the outside to present a fat offer to show them what they were worth. Selling the company gave them that, but it was a very harsh answer to that need to know the value of something you had created, because they also gave up control.

I have forged the financial and labor relationships that have saved companies from ruin. I have worked with unions all over the world.

I know that the most powerful management tool we can carry with us has little to do with finance, with business systems, with structure, with technology. There is no doubt about the importance of those parts of the formula. But without trust that spreads all across a company, a sense that everyone shares in the glory and the gloom, even the best performance in those other areas will not deliver success. World competition is too tough to accept the basic inefficiency of internal labor-management disharmony.

We entered the twentieth century firmly cemented in an us versus them mode. If we are to succeed in the next century, as managers, as workers, and as owners, that distinction must be banished.

I know this beast of distrust particularly well because it comes to visit so often.

It was sitting right on my desk just before I retired from United.

United was losing qualified airport and reservations employees due to more competitive salaries in the airline industry. I knew the solution. I wanted to give them more money. I was well aware that we were behind the curve on pay, one of the realities that happened when United Airlines shifted to employee ownership six years ago.

The workers gave up salary in exchange for a big piece of the action. We had a plan to solve that problem, but it was designed to play out over time. Those workers needed the money immediately. They were valuable to us and they deserved it.

Why couldn't I give it to them?

The simple answer was that I was not trusted.

It was a lesson for me in how deep the historical taproot runs in unions, and in management, too. No matter how hard you try to remedy the faults of the past, unions remain unions.

But I can't accept the assumption that nothing ever really changes. We live in history's only truly flexible, expandable, portable culture. The bad side of that is reflected in the foolish way the culture exploits art and music, the appeal to the darker sides of our nature. The best side of it is our acceptance of wave after wave of immigration, and our willingness to constantly reinvent ourselves.

No one is in control of the Internet, for example. It is the great leveler in our culture. But how can that experience be incorporated in unions? One way is to recognize that information is now available to everyone, including all union members. So it is less likely now that a small, vocal minority could influence the choice of union leaders. Still, it happens.

What that means is that union leadership is constantly looking for ways to strengthen its position, and the easiest tool at hand is to demonize management. But that is old thinking that damages any chance for a new relationship between managers and the people who work with them.

My hope is that the Internet will lead to a greater democratization of unions, so that an informed membership will have more control over the behavior of its leaders.

But I wasn't seeing much of that as we battled over my attempt to give more money to our employees.

It was a very unusual situation.

Typically, when unions and management sit across a bargaining table, management wants to pay less and the union wants to get more. In this case, the situation was reversed.

I had a solution. Because everyone was going through a transition as we became employee-owned, I suggested we just raise their pay. I was satisfied to let the union take credit for the move, because I needed higher salaries to attract and keep qualified people.

But the unions resisted. They were concerned initially that if United simply raised the salaries, the employees would lose their interest in joining the union. The way the union viewed the situation, lower salaries were in its interest for the time being, because that would help encourage union membership.

The union would not allow me to give employees the salary increases that I should have used to keep them working at United. Instead, we had to follow the time-tested formula of contract negotiations and ratification. That meant many months would pass before their salaries could be increased.

What happened because of that?

United undoubtedly lost a lot of good employees to other airlines and better opportunities. Customer service suffered. That damaged the company and cost money as new workers were hired and trained. We almost certainly lost customers, too, because they felt they were not being properly treated. The perception of the gap between management and labor would be reinforced.

I understand why this happened, but I certainly wish there were something I could say, or do, to change it.

But the problem is apparent, and has many layers.

Unions are reluctant to cooperate to solve grievances before they become formal, because quiet solutions don't give them the visibility that they would win during a formal grievance procedure.

They won't talk to management about plans for hard times that would involve management and labor salary cuts.

No one is willing to sit down and tell management: "Here is what we don't like and if you start doing it, we will jump all over you. But in the meantime, we'll get out of your way—no restrictive labor contracts. Go make money and grow the company."

I had my own particular goal for employee relations at United.

I was intrigued by *Fortune* magazine's annual survey of companies that people most want to work for. I kept asking myself, "How do I get United Airlines on that list?"

I didn't make it.

We started our campaign to get on that list in my fourth year as CEO.

We even spent time with the author who does the selecting to understand what he found in the companies he chose. We searched for ideas we could emulate.

He had some solid advice. The most important thing, he said, was for a company to be highly profitable. That surprised me, but it makes sense. Who wants to go to work for a company that is losing money? But he said you can't buy your way into this kind of employee group. You have to be seen as fair. He talked about respect and what that really meant.

He told us that with hard work and consistency, it might take five years to make the list. We had a good start on the project by the time I retired, but United still had a long way to go.

As unusual as it might seem, my own ideas about organized labor were not formed in the corporate suite.

I am most certainly not a modern robber baron. Scratch my surface and what you find, deep down, is a kid from St. Louis whose values and background come from a liberal political tradition that put organized labor right up on a pedestal. That is why this question of trust is such a per-

plexing problem for me. I know where distrust comes
from.

When I came on board, I reached out to some veterans
for advice on how I should handle my new job at United.
These were mostly retired union people, and they gave me
a list of dos and don'ts.

Don't wear red suspenders, they said, because that will
remind people at United Airlines of Steve Wolf. Don't wear
a cowboy hat. Same reason. But more to the point, don't
ever say "Trust me." If you say that, I was told, you will call
up fifteen years of nasty memories of how it was before you
arrived.

I kept asking our people when they would be able to
judge this management on the basis of its own behavior,
not on the basis of the people who ran this company before. They got increasingly uncomfortable when I talked
that way, but they were still not willing to put us to that
test.

I know where this animosity comes from, on both sides.
I understand that management has a bad track record on
labor issues. I don't think I would have any trouble at all
writing this book from labor's perspective. But I also understand that times change and people change.

I don't want to be a slave to that history. I didn't want
United Airlines to be a slave to that history, and I don't
think the rest of corporate America and organized labor
should be trapped by history, either.

So, irony of ironies, there I was in my last months at
United, wrestling with organized labor and its behaviors,
sometimes cast as an enemy, but, in fact, sympathetic to the
value of unions.

In a way, I am still standing in that stairwell, but the message is different this time.

The American labor movement is in trouble, and some
of the issues are glaring. Our nation's standard of living is
obviously better because of unions, but union membership

keeps dropping. Without a major reversal, the union movement will lose its importance in America and we will all suffer for it.

At the same time, the type of resurgent effort we see in unions today is a shift back to the old ways.

I watched the demonstrations during the World Trade Organization's Seattle meeting in late 1999. The unions were lining up against a WTO which was encouraging free trade with countries that might have bad practices with regard to the environment and labor standards.

My message is simple.

Work for unionization in the countries where the abuses have occurred. And if those nations refuse to allow unionization, then turn to the government for some leverage. But don't expect Washington to unionize and establish high labor standards in other countries.

Why should organized labor want prescriptions for the future from a lifelong manager? Because I don't think the level of reconstruction I am calling for can happen from one side. We simply can't construct a successful future unless we do it together.

If management continues to play the role established so long ago, then it will collect nothing but a harvest of trouble from its employees. If labor continues to view management as a target rather than as a partner, it, too, will miss out on the unprecedented opportunities presented by globalization.

I think the problem these days is that unions are just about as insular as too many corporate managers.

Suggestions, complaints, criticism from the outside, unions want nothing of it.

Let me give you an example.

Unionizing at United Airlines was a complicated business. There were provisions in labor law, with the signing of membership cards that would allow the CEO to recognize a union and instruct workers to be members. But there are also provisions for setting up an election to determine union representation.

In 1998, one union wanted to represent a collection of nineteen thousand nonunion workers at United. But what that union wanted was a decision from the airline to accept the union and put it in place. They argued that they had cards signed by a majority of workers.

My point was that simply declaring that union as the representative would be bad for the union and bad for United, too. How would it look to our workers if management declared a union to be on board and cut off any other option?

I think the union's assumption was that the management wanted an election so we could turn to that old management play book and try to beat the union out of an election victory. I thought United's people would revolt if they were required to start paying dues without an election.

I understand where those union attitudes come from. Management helped create them. For many years, managers all over the country—and at United, too—have been using that management play book to undercut unionization attempts.

I'm not saying that some management people shouldn't be demonized.

After all, they've earned it.

In our own case, I was trying to handle the issue in a different way, though. I wasn't just demanding an election, although that is what I have always believed in. I thought democracy was the strongest tool in those situations. After all, it is our own American heritage. People have to make their own decisions.

Of United's 90,000 employees in 1997, some 35,000 were not in unions. The issue at hand covered nineteen thousand employees, most of them clerical and customer contact people. I told the union that management would not recommend whether they should join the union or not. I said we would do our best to get the facts out, and that would be the extent of our role.

I was not being disingenuous. My view was that all of our employees were owners, including those who were not in unions. My belief is that management should create conditions in which employees don't feel they need a third party to represent them.

But if employees feel that condition does not exist, then the choice to unionize or not is theirs. It is too late at that point for management to come up with a wonderful new plan. The decision rests with the employees.

Management's job is to keep the record straight. During this struggle, for example, the union claimed that if there was another employee stock ownership program, nonunion members would be cut out of the approval process. We set the record straight on that. This management, we said, promised that if there is a new ESOP, your group will determine your involvement and management will be guided by that decision.

The bitterness connected with that experience is softening now. Frankly, I think that is because the union won the election by 53 percent, but not because they believed I was right about any of it. I hope the next time an opportunity for unionization comes along, that old knee-jerk reaction will not be repeated, but I have my doubts.

There are some signals managers should pay attention to when unionization efforts come along. The first is that a push to unionize is a vote of no confidence in management. It might not be personal, but it certainly is a warning about a deep lack of trust between workers and management.

It may seem an uncomfortable responsibility, but it is management's job to provide the right work environment and pay. To the extent that management tries to pay below-market wages, it is just asking for trouble from workers. These are economic issues created by management, and can be solved by management.

In that sense, the push to unionize isn't any different from any relationship in the world, including a marriage. Here is what is being said: "I don't trust you enough that you and I can talk things out one on one. I want an intermediary."

As a manager, you can't duck that because it says something about you. I think management has to be much more self-critical about its role. If people want to unionize, it is because management is not doing its job to represent employees, to be their steward, to think through what managers must do to earn employee loyalty and trust.

Strong differences, even frequent strikes, could be absorbed in the narrow economy of the 1950s. It is a different matter when everyone competes on the world stage. That is a condition that requires unity of purpose.

The playing field has literally expanded to reach every corner of the world. The customer has choices across the globe and will not pay for your inefficiencies, family spats, or other similar nonsense.

As a related matter, economic protectionism simply can't work anymore. Of course management or unions can create an atmosphere where they have political clout through campaign contributions, and you can get the workers excited about the subject. You can even force the government to take a protectionist attitude for an industry. But that sets up a false relationship between an industry and the world it must compete in.

Consumers want quality products at competitive prices. If they are given the choice between an American-made television at a price that reflects the higher cost of U.S. labor and an imported television that sells at a deep discount because it can be made more efficiently offshore, we already know what option the U.S. consumer will pursue.

The economics of that formula are so dominant that they outweigh anything that gets in the way. If consumers wanted to pay higher prices for U.S.-made televisions, there would be a booming U.S. television market today.

A better goal would be productivity improvements, and there are two policies a company can institute to encourage them. The first is to share ownership with employees through compensation and stock programs.

Owners take their work more seriously than employees, who may feel distant from the true interests of a company. Try to create a no-layoffs environment so workers have a strong sense of security. And if you do need to lower the employee population, do it over time by using attrition.

The message the unions must understand is that quality and price earn the loyalty of customers in the long run. Building walls around institutions only isolates them from the inevitable changes that dominate the real world outside.

Virtually every other institution has not only accepted that reality, but also embraced it.

Only the unions were fighting the North American Free Trade Agreement, for example. The unions define the issue in terms of jobs shifting from their own turf in the United States to someone else's turf in another country. But NAFTA was only a political response to the reality that is already dominating the world marketplace.

As controversial as NAFTA was, it was a late entry in a game that was already under way. There were enormous cracks in the walls of protectionism among and between Canada, the United States, and Mexico. U.S. car companies were already working in an atmosphere that allowed them to put their factories wherever they wanted in the United States or Canada.

And the Mexican government had already created a system that allowed American companies to ship semi-finished products into Mexico for final assembly and ship finished products back to the United States without duty charges.

Denying those realities would not have changed them.

Unions should also recognize the importance of the word "international" in their titles and start expanding unionization efforts around the world. The message is that the turf of the union can be vastly expanded, from the

American factories and workplaces of the 1950s and 1960s
to the factories of the world as a new century dawns.

Too many unions seem to see their international role as
trying to push the U.S. government to tell Mexico or Thai-
land not to employ people under poor working conditions.
I think it is wrong for people to work under those conditions, too. It is wrong for them to be exploited and to face
constant threats in the workplace.

But organized labor hasn't even scratched the surface of
this issue. They have not begun to deal with the tough
questions. Unionizing the mines and workplaces in the
United States was hard work, and it will be hard work to
bring unionization to the rest of the developing world, too.
But they have to start working diligently at this challenge.

How can they find a way to build the trust to unionize
workers in other countries?

Start with a notion. Do the easy ones first.

Go to the workers of American companies and American company suppliers outside the United States. U.S.
unions have the best shot at success there. Look for the
conditions that create the need and the alliances among
workers that can be used to plant the seeds of an expanded, internationalized union movement.

Corporate CEOs may wince at this idea, but we get free
trade in the bargain. And remember, we should not respond to unions the way our predecessors did in the 1930s.

Although most U.S. unions have the word "international" in their titles and have a token membership outside
the country, there is only one union I am aware of that has
membership outside the United States other than Canada,
and that is the Association of Flight Attendants. United Airlines has the right to employ flight attendants from all over
the world who are not U.S. citizens, but they have to be
paid the same, no matter where they live. The fringe benefits may be different because of various government pension and health programs, but the base pay is the same,

whether a flight attendant lives in New York, Hong Kong, Paris or London or Santiago.

United goes offshore for employment, but not because it wants to save money. United needs culture and language skills because our passengers are from all over the world. I think this is a sign of an opportunity for unionization on a worldwide basis. The framework is already there.

Another reality affects this emerging world-scale playing field for unions, too.

Employment in manufacturing is going downhill in the U.S. and is going to continue to go downhill, probably for the next twenty to twenty-five years because of new technology. Think of what happened to the farm sector in the United States over the past century. That is likely to happen to manufacturing, too. Because of extraordinary efficiency and technology, 3 or 4 percent of our workforce cannot only feed the U.S., but feed some of the rest of the world, too.

At the turn of the century, it took most of the people of the United States to provide the nation's food supply. Draw the comparison yourself. Manufacturing is 14 percent of our workforce today and dropping year by year.

What does this mean for unions?

They can isolate and insulate themselves from these realities and eventually they will simply dry up. Or they can recognize the significance of the shift and the speed with which the world is changing, and they can change with it.

Unions need to recognize this before it is too late, but there aren't enough signs they do, or that they are willing to change quickly.

The signs that the message is finally getting through will be union recognition of the importance and value of free trade across the world, and recognition that the United States is a competitive place that creates good products. That will increase employment.

Finally, union leaders will be measured by the objective goals they set. When they do that, it will probably mean an increase in the turnover at the top of unions, but that kind of change will be healthy.

The primary audience for unionization these days is the service worker in the service industry, more and more the white-collar worker, and perhaps even more important, the woman in the workplace.

The bulk of our society no longer works in isolated, protected industries represented by factories and production lines. A century ago, the people who built the union movement recognized that the population of the United States was moving from the countryside to the city, and more important, moving to the factories and the mines and the railroads of America to work.

Service is where the growth is, and manufacturing is slowly shrinking. Union leadership knows this but progress is too slow.

I suspect that is because they are applying old methods to new challenges.

Of course the union movement has work to do at home, too, and that calls for some rethinking of those traditional roles. Corporate America has been opening the door (reluctantly) to union representation on its boards of directors for decades now. Why doesn't that particular road go both ways?

If unions recognize the value of having their own members on corporate boards, why can't they see the value of having corporate representatives serving on labor councils?

A corporate representative on a labor council would understand that the people running the union must be accountable and must establish goals. People with corporate experience know all about recruiting for new leaders and members. And most corporate folks are comfortable in international commerce and could help unions become truly international.

Best of all, corporate people are good at hammering out five-year plans and holding people to them.

I am not lobbying for the job. There are at least a hundred people in corporate America who would be fair but tough-minded and who would push union councils hard enough to make their eyes roll, the same way some of the union representatives make corporate eyes roll on boards of directors now.

I saw an example of this problem in another form last year.

I was in a meeting and we were struggling with the question of what our employees want and believe about the value of extending the ownership structure at United Airlines. This would require buying more shares of stock after the year 2000, when the current plan expires.

Instead of guessing or dictating a solution, one of the union leaders at the meeting said, "Well, why don't we just have the two key unions and management put their heads together and agree on a survey and hire a third party to conduct it? Then they could come back and tell us the results and we would know how people feel about the issue."

There was immediate resistance from another union leader.

"No way," he said. "I know what my people want, and the last thing I would do is cooperate with management to do the survey."

On one level, that old lack of trust was apparent. On another level, the union leader at that session did not want to be seen as the kind of character who would cooperate with management in any way.

I was encouraged as a new younger and more modern-thinking group of folks was beginning to emerge in this union, a hopeful sign for the future.

These kinds of attitudes still exist on the management side, too.

There are still corporate characters who claim they know what consumers and employees want and resist conducting surveys.

Maybe they are afraid of the answers.

These problems pop up with such amazing frequency, even at a progressive company like United, that I view them as clear warnings about the need for a change in attitude.

For example, I tried to convince the unions at United to take a more active role in the running of the business. For almost five years, I invited United's unions to take a much more active role in long-term planning.

The Air Line Pilots Association seized the opportunity to engage in the business of United, both in strategic planning discussions, safety planning, and a whole range of business-related issues. On the other hand, the International Association of Machinists did not even want to come to these sessions. I think that was because the union was having a difficult time breaking away from its own blue-collar image, although the new machinists union leadership is changing.

The flight attendant union participated on the margins. They have so much education and experience, but it seems to me that they are reluctant to tap it. I was concerned that they viewed the invitation primarily as an opportunity to acquire intelligence for union negotiations.

What would I tell a young union leader about leadership?

1. Don't reject criticism. It is not a sign of anti-unionism. Everyone else in the business formula is learning about the value of constructive criticism. The same process should be under way inside unions.
2. Be aware of what it means that business is becoming global.
3. Internationalize your union.
4. Put businesspeople on union councils.
5. Try management by objective.

I grew up in an ethnic minority group that has consistently resisted being painted with the same brush all the time. But that is what this union attitude toward management involves, an assumption that all managers were born with a silver spoon in their mouths. You know the old line, "He was born on third base and thinks he hit a triple!"

I would recommend the union leader of the future struggle to defeat that kind of attitude.

Most of all, I would recommend that it is the union's obligation to understand business. That way, the union can understand the need for developing rules and compensation structures that work in everyone's interest.

They don't really need to know what managers spend most of their lives studying. But they do need to know enough about the goals and objectives of business to find ways to help meet them.

I have advice, too, for the thirty-year-old manager who is headed for the CEO's office and who wants to know how to deal with labor unions and employees:

1. Represent employees so well that they do not feel the need to bring in a third party to protect them.
2. Be strictly neutral on the question of unionization.
3. Give the employees the facts and then let them have their election.
4. Recognize that union officials are obliged to satisfy their membership. Understand their needs.
5. Encourage union members to understand the business they are in.
6. Use effective communication, openness, and honesty to rebuild trust.
7. If irreconcilable differences between management and employees come up, employee ownership can be a great change agent.

Then I would put that young executive in a time machine and take her back to St. Louis and the stairwell to talk about the lessons of history and what they tell us about the need for change.

★

TEN

Leave Your Old Ethics at the Door: Ours Are Better

I got one of my most practical lessons in handling ethical questions in Venezuela, where I was running the Ford Motor Co. subsidiary. I loved the country and the people. But it was inevitable I would run into a conflict that is common for Americans who work in other countries.

The problem was corruption, and the challenge was to find some way to deal with it that wouldn't damage my company and would not violate my own ethical code of behavior.

It was an early lesson in ethics for me, but I have handled ethical issues at just about every level on too many continents to count. My experience has taught me that the questions of ethics don't start or stop with corrupt business practices in foreign countries.

In many cases, ethical issues don't focus on questions of corruption at all.

Much more important is the question of ethical behavior toward one another in the workplace. We attacked that problem at United Airlines and came up with our own statement of ethical behaviors, which we called "Rules of the Road." In a way, these rules have their roots in my experience in Venezuela, and the thoughts and reactions that flowed from trying to deal ethically with a corrupt situation.

I believe that definition of ethics—how you deal with the

people you work with, and how they deal with you—is at the heart of business relationships and affects everyone every day.

There are some ugly people in corporate America and their version of getting on with their own career is to compete, ruthlessly, with their colleagues.

That sounds like a pretty harsh assessment, doesn't it?

But it is also accurate. It amazes me that so much of American business still embraces tainted values that are so damaging to everyone's interests.

It's not as though I invented this thought at the beginning of my career. I learned about it watching the best people do their jobs well, and the worst people do their jobs quite badly.

I know how it feels to work for someone who views the entire universe in his own terms, who cannot stand to be challenged or surrounded by creative people who just might have more to contribute than he recognizes.

I loved competing in both track and football when I was a young man.

One required superior individual skills, the other a team that worked well together.

Anyone who cares more about himself in football than he cares about the team will damage the effort. You might win the game, but the results just aren't going to be as good as they would be if the importance of teamwork were recognized.

There is no separation between personal ethics and business ethics, and that is a lesson I started to learn in the ethical wilds of Venezuela, when a big decision was on the table, and palms were facing up looking to be greased.

The government of Venezuela decided at one point that all cars being assembled in Venezuela should choose from only two engines.

It was a terrible idea, but it presented a substantial opportunity for the two companies that ultimately would win the contracts. It was my goal to convince the Venezuelan government that this just wasn't the right way to go. But I wasn't having a lot of luck.

At one point, I met with a businessperson to discuss the engines project. It was pointed out, quite clearly, that a lot of money was at stake. With the right "encouragement," Ford could get one of the engine contracts.

In short, he wanted a bribe.

I was forty-one, full of vinegar and eager to do well. But I could smell trouble from the minute I heard the proposal.

If this had been a movie, the American hero would have jumped right up and shouted, "You slimy bastard!"

But you don't dare say things like that when you are doing business in another culture. I had already learned that the society in Venezuela was terribly corrupt.

And I had already decided I wasn't going to play that game.

In the first place, I was working for a company that had high ethical standards. In the second place, there was a new U.S. law in effect, the Anti-Corrupt Practices Act, that sent a clear warning that the U.S. Department of Justice was not going to look kindly on overseas bribery, no matter what the local atmosphere.

How does an executive handle a request for a bribe?

I developed my own method, and it was based on the thought that these kinds of problems would have to be handled tactfully. It simply would not do for the head of Ford in Venezuela to ride in on a high horse lecturing the locals about U.S. ethical standards.

I had to find another way, a response that would not offend my host, but also that would not put Ford or me in jeopardy.

The more responsibility you have in a corporation, the more you must learn to keep your own counsel. I am not recommending dishonesty at any level. But I do believe you must pick your spots well to speak out and remember that everyone is watching you.

What did I do?

Reforming Venezuelan society was not my responsibility. Protecting the values of American business culture was very much my responsibility. So I searched for a way to resolve the issue without yielding to the demand for a bribe.

I told the Venezuelan businessman I simply didn't have the money in my budget for that kind of activity and that if I spent it, it would stick out and be obvious. I told him I was sorry but I couldn't do it.

And that solved the bribery problem.

As for the engine project, ultimately I joined with some others in persuading the government it was a mistake.

I look back on my own career, what I achieved and how I achieved it. I believe I had a most pleasant ride and I think that I helped the companies that I worked for. I had my own rule for survival and success inside corporations.

It is easy to describe, but difficult to achieve.

My goal was always to get my boss promoted.

That has always worked a lot better for me than just pushing for my own advancement, even at Ford Motor Co., which was run by Henry Ford II during my term there.

Let's be realistic. Whose name was on the company headquarters?

There was one man at the top and everyone else was far down the pecking order.

If you deconstruct Lee Iacocca's departure from Ford, you will immediately understand the process. There could only be one king of the hill at that company, and it wasn't going to be Iacocca, no matter how well he designed and marketed automobiles.

I realized during my years at Ford that the closer one moved to the top, the closer one got to the throne, the more apparent it was that one man was running the company.

This was the imperial presidency transferred to the world of business. Mentioning the name "Henry Ford" alone was enough in many situations.

I saw entire divisions of the company stop in their tracks simply to devote all their attention to preparing for a visit from the man at the top.

I never let that atmosphere get in the way of my own philosophy, even though at times it transformed me into a tour guide and travel agent. I knew I had a lot to learn at Ford, and I knew how important it would be to create relationships that would continue my education.

I worked for a time as the administrative assistant to Ford's small-car chief engineer. My goal was to get my job done and get him promoted. His reward for getting a quality car done on time was a promotion to chief engineer for Ford of Europe.

Here was a man who had no college education, but who did his job so well he became the chief engineer of Europe. It was amazing. I am not taking credit for his promotion, but I helped him. It came naturally for me.

People respond when you do that. They are not on their guard.

As a young executive, I found that this attitude meant folks were interested in serving as my mentor; they were relaxed around me. It worked well for my career, too. I moved from engineering into the controller's office, where I had a different assignment every six months. I learned a lot about the financial side of car building, and I learned a lot about the silliness of corporations, too.

I recall working for a man who thought he had come up with the perfect formula to get what he wanted inside the corporation. Anyone who has spent much time in the corporate suite has run into this kind of character. They believe they are masters of their own narrow universe. You see this kind of attitude play out a lot at budget time.

This particular manager sent me a proposal to add six hundred employees to his organization. I got the first shot at analyzing the plan. I concluded that what he actually needed was two people.

So I went to talk to him about it.

I asked him, "What is this? You only need two people. Why are you asking for six hundred?"

He told me he was never going to admit he needed only two people. The thought of being honest about the request had never entered his mind. He was going to play the game the Ford way.

"In this company of ours," he said, "if you ever need just two people, then ask for six hundred, because there are going to be ten guys just like you, and each of you is responsible for whittling me down. So if I ask for what I want, you will give me less. It's up to you to figure out what I need."

It was nonsense, but I saw it playing out all of the time.

One assignment at Ford painted a very accurate picture of what was wrong then, and probably still stands as an accurate picture of what is wrong in a lot of businesses today. We were facing a big meeting on financial issues. It would be at headquarters, known as the Glass House.

The number two man at the division called my controller, Sev Vass. The number two man had a southern accent, so you have to imagine this conversation taking place somewhere in Georgia.

I can still hear it today.

"Sev," he said, "I got to go to one of them meetings up there at the Glass House. You better go find out how many of them young financial boys they are going to bring to that meeting and how many of them black books they are going to have, and you make sure you send along with me more of our financial boys with more of them black books than they have."

His assumption was they were going to eat him alive.

Sev Vass was very smart.

He was great at convincing headquarters that, even though we were asking for more, it was really less than anyone should expect. He taught me how to do it. You would start by saying, "Now, here is what we had last year. Now let me make adjustments for conditions."

And no matter how he got there, he always ended up with more than last year.

Of course, it made no sense at all, but it worked at Ford.

Sev got rewarded for helping the head of the division explain the numbers and I got rewarded for helping him.

It was ridiculous, but at least Sev could laugh at himself. With most of the rest of these guys, it was real bullets.

Remember the world of business in that era.

Harold Geneen was revered at ITT; he created that company.

He was all work all the time. Built ITT from $700 million in annual sales to billions.

One of his favorite management practices was to call his division heads into meetings and chew their butts, as publicly as he could. He would have six or seven of his own staff people on board as witnesses and then he would just chew people up and down.

He would always be smarter.

He would always have some angle.

All meetings had to be held on his time. He would show up in Brussels for a meeting and it would be midnight, Brussels time, but that's when the meeting started because he wanted everything to work on his own schedule. Everyone would stay awake for his meetings, or try to.

That was the model of managerial success for that era.

Unfortunately, the model still sounds familiar.

One step beyond meritocracy in a corporation is ugliness.

That was why it was frequently so difficult at Ford. I would spend 80 percent of my sixteen-hour day negotiating with people inside the company instead of spending 80 percent of my time figuring out how to make cars and get them sold.

I wanted to be in a battle with my real competitors, but

I found myself wrapped up in skirmishes inside my own company.

That was not unusual in corporations in those days and I don't think it is unusual today. My bet would be that you could find lots of corporations that have the same problems Ford had four decades ago. They have created a hyper-competitive internal environment, and it is damaging them.

Look at Arthur Andersen. There is no reason for Andersen's management consultants to be fighting with Andersen's accountants. They have created this gigantic pie, an enormous pie, but they are spending their time fighting over who is going to have the biggest piece of it.

Everyone with any sense recognizes how damaging these attitudes can be.

I showed up at United in 1994 after the airline had been through three or four years of wrenching turmoil. I believe the former management was trying to scare the hell out of the employees. The company was losing money. The managers decided to become demons who would shrink the company through layoffs.

That created an extraordinary stress on the officers of the company. My goal was to try to nudge the company into the new world of consensus management, and the Rules of the Road would provide the map for that journey.

We were going to help people help themselves.

I turned to Dino Baris, a Chicago psychiatrist who had been the adviser to the Air Line Pilots Association.

He gave the pilots a most practical example of what employee ownership would mean to them. He took their leaders to a restaurant and, after lunch, he suggested they strike themselves in the face. They wanted to know exactly why he would expect them to do that in public. They pointed out they had no earthly reason to strike themselves.

"Exactly," he said. "That is the point."

After his experience with the pilots, Baris approached us

and said he thought the whole company could benefit if it could develop a sense of teamwork.

What United needed then, and what a lot of other corporations need today, is a standard of ethical behavior that works. That is the need that led us to the Rules of the Road.

It wasn't sufficient simply to warn everyone to abide by the laws and shun bribery overseas. The ethical problem I sensed was much closer to home. It had its roots in the way people dealt with one another every day.

Lots of companies have ethics policies or standards of behavior.

The problem is that they amount to little more than words printed on handy little cards or on wall posters. Companies draft these policies, print them up, and then forget to apply them.

I think it is important that a company has a statement of ethical behavior written down, but it can't just be something that fills a block on some executive's checklist. I wanted employees at United to understand that their ethics in church on Sunday should be the same as they are at work on Monday.

Very few companies take the time to understand the importance of ethics in day-to-day working relationships. Most CEOs don't realize that it is their job, and probably their top job.

I would argue that ethical behavior is not an abstraction glued to the bottom of a company's mission statement. It is a living, breathing responsibility that dictates how people relate to one another every day. It presents an opportunity to create a better company.

How do people in your company relate to one another on a day-to-day basis? I have had experience with a lot of different models over the past few decades.

I recall a sign I once saw over the front gate of a company in Northern Ireland. It told the workers to leave their politics at the door. That warning reflected one company's way of trying to deal with an outside problem that could have been devastating had it played out inside.

My version today would say: "Leave your outside ethics at the door, because we have better ones inside."

I know that sounds a little unusual, but it is a conclusion I reached after watching these kinds of problems play out everywhere from Ford Motor to investment banks and to United Airlines.

I remember thinking about this at Ford during my early days, back in the late 1950s. One of my bosses was complaining about the fact that he spent so much of his time fighting with other people inside Ford that he wasn't able to spend much time at all paying attention to business. I doubt that is a problem at Ford today, but it certainly was when I joined the company.

Ford was a meritocracy in the extreme. I didn't want to play that game, but it was apparent to me that a lot of what went on at Ford was the scramble of individuals trying to make themselves look good.

Sometimes, that meant making your likely competitor inside the company look bad. That whole process was draining and got in the way of what we were actually supposed to be doing—making and selling automobiles.

I learned early on there were two ways that chief executive officers and boards of directors figured out who was going to be promoted. For some, they established an early plan and stuck with it. Over time, they let people know who was going to fit in. But other companies took a much different approach.

I call it putting tigers in the cage, and it is one of the most common and damaging of modern business practices.

The objective was to put several tigers in a cage and see who survived.

That was the Ford style in the 1950s, and in my view it was counterproductive. If you collect a bunch of Type A personalities inside a company and unleash that kind of attitude, pretty soon teams form up underneath them, and that causes territorial turf battles all over the company. It is exactly what you don't want if your goal is to encourage teamwork.

The situation was different at Chrysler.

Chrysler was a collection of renegades.

But we were united by the fact that we were involved in an industrial war. We had a company that was just about dead, and we worked hard for several years to bring it back to life. That bonded us to one another and turned us into a genuine team. I believe that 80 percent, maybe 90 percent of the people at Chrysler felt that way about one another.

That was remarkable, because Lee Iacocca's tendency was to put those tigers in the cage and let them fight it out. That worked at the time, but what it meant is that there were a lot of hungry tigers stalking about after Chrysler had saved itself and started making money.

I don't believe that either Ford or Chrysler had anything written down that would provide guidelines for behavior. Of course there were rule books, and technical manuals, but they were for specialists. There was nothing you could point to that defined how those places worked, how people related to one another.

In that sense, Dillon Read was a good experience for me, even though I never really took to investment banking.

Wall Street looked upon Dillon Read as one of those white shoe kinds of places that had history and ethics dictated by behaviors over a long period of time. It was very much the Princeton sense of ethics playing out inside a business, and that felt comfortable for me. (Princeton has had a long-standing and serious honors system. You don't cheat, and you blow the whistle on those who do.)

That wasn't the case with some of the other investment banks, though. Sometimes hyperbole defines that business, and I have always felt that was dishonest. The goal seemed to be to promise the sky in the most positive of terms, despite the realities of the individual case.

Many were sophisticated salesmen and not shy at all about marching right up to the edge of the ethical cliff.

And sometimes a few of them wouldn't hesitate to jump right off the edge.

I think there are other kinds of unethical behaviors afoot in modern business, too, and I saw a good example of it at the Czech truck company I was trying to rebuild. For almost half a century, the workers had been taught that they should not show any incentive. It was a legacy of all those years of communist control.

Whatever you said to them, you had to say literally, because they were going to follow it to the letter. No one would march an inch beyond the clearly established game plan. There was no out-of-the-box thinking, and certainly no behavior aimed at improving performance or standards.

You see the same situation in some American companies today. This is a particular problem in unionized companies where bitterness leads everyone to work exactly to the rule.

The challenge of modern management, then, is to recognize these realities and find a way to inject responsibilities along with rights for employees.

I think we were in the vanguard of addressing workplace ethics at United Airlines, but we didn't get there haphazardly. I don't want to imply that all of United's problems are solved. That clearly is not the case. But we constructed some operating standards and principles of behavior that set the mark for our employees and managers.

We built our Rules of the Road from the ground up over an intensive, six-month period of study, thought, and conversation. Frankly, I got a little tired of the process at some points. I suppose that was just my Type A personality asserting itself. People would talk endlessly in meetings about changing this word or that, or trying to find a clearer way to send the message.

It took that Chicago psychiatrist, Dino Baris, to help us work it out.

Baris, perceptive, highly persuasive, and informal at the same time, knew what we needed and he knew where the problems were. But before we even started typing up versions of the rules, we needed a basic understanding, crucial to the process.

Everyone involved had to know we weren't kidding.

I told the executives at United early on that we shouldn't develop these rules and then just post them on a wall. I told them I was going to hold them accountable. The officers had to live by these standards we were creating. And I warned them that, after some experience with the rules, if I found some officers who were not in compliance, they would need to find other employment.

At United, I told everyone the Rules of the Road would be an all-or-nothing proposition. I believe that set the tone for what followed. Getting everyone to take the whole process seriously was the first hurdle. Once we had agreed on that, we were ready to go.

But first we had to change some attitudes. We had to relearn how to run meetings, for example. We had to establish ways to resolve disagreements between executives. We had to define what we meant when we said we were all obliged to deliver complete and impartial information.

What we found out, over time, was that some executives simply couldn't do it. They were command and control experts who would have been valuable at certain kinds of companies, but not at the United we were trying to construct. So we offered them good financial packages and encouraged them to leave. Four or five of them took us up on our offer.

We started the Rules of the Road with an introduction that pointed out that we meant exactly what we were saying. We told our employees and our executives that our goal was to contribute to the efficiency of the company and to be able to enjoy our jobs more.

Here they are.

Rule One:
Place the Team's Interest Before My Own

We were trying to make an important point. We wanted everyone to understand that if their agenda involved back-stabbing for personal advancement, United Airlines was going to pay the price. In that kind of atmosphere, people are distracted from the business at hand by their own self-interest.

I saw that problem at Ford long before we sat down to hammer out United's rules. One of my bosses became angry with me after I had given some information to someone outside the department who used it later in a meeting. My boss was upset because he said it made him look bad that the other person presented information at the meeting that helped everyone arrive at a better decision.

Rule Two:
Listen Fully and Respect Each Individual

Sounds simple, doesn't it? But listening fully and with respect isn't easy, particularly when you are in a room full of Type As who might be more interested in presenting their own agendas and advancing their own causes.

This second rule involved a lesson from my own casebook. In my youth, I was so eager that I would frequently interrupt people during meetings. I knew something was wrong when one of my favorite bosses at Ford, Ed Molina, told me to be quiet and let another person finish his statement.

Rule Three:
Speak with Candor and Honesty

This is the "no bullshit" rule.

It tells folks they should not talk unless they know what they are going to say. Don't waste everyone's time. Coming from St. Louis, I have my own version: Be Midwestern. To my mind, that means being direct and honest.

I recall a marketing session with a key consultant at United. The pro who knew about this part of the business was ill, so the company sent a substitute who decided he would fill the time with nonsense and generalities. The consulting company got into real trouble with me for doing that. It takes knowledge to present a point with candor and honesty. A meeting room is no place for vamping.

You must always set the scene so people understand why they are in the room. Defining some terms—what kind of a meeting it is, for example—helps.

At a unilateral meeting, the context is this: "I'm telling you what I have decided and I expect everyone to live by it."

At a consultative meeting, I am going to listen to everyone in the room. We might even take an official vote on a question. And then I am going to decide, based on these consultations.

The third one is collaborative, a fancy term that means we are all equals in this room. On the question at hand, it means we are not going to decide anything until we have a consensus of all the people in the room.

The kind of meeting we are having might not always be clear to everyone, but I have found under our Rules of the Road that people at United ask if they don't understand. It is not unusual to hear someone pipe up: "Could we get clear what kind of a meeting this is?"

Rule Four:
Include All Who Have a Stake in an Issue

No one should feel shut out of a conversation, I mean a conversation that deals directly with that person's responsibilities. This one is a hard standard to meet, but you have to work at it. You cannot get a team of people to work toward an objective unless everyone affected has had a chance to express their views before a decision is made.

I saw one of those situations at Chrysler. I was part of a group that developed a plan for a new model. We worked out everything, and then we brought the sales guys in. They went crazy! They said the dealers would revolt under those circumstances. The sales people should have been involved from the beginning.

Rule Five:
Provide Complete and Impartial Information

How many times have you gone to a meeting with knowledge in your head only to hold something back? Or how many times have you colored information to send a different message? Or how many times have you left something out that was central to the task? How many times have you gone to a meeting unprepared?

This one says just what it means. I like to think of it in terms of old-time journalism. The news pages were for facts, well and clearly presented. The editorial pages were for opinion. News calls for a full and fair treatment of reality. The editorial pages allow leeway in what is said or not said.

Just the facts, all the facts, and the facts as free of opinion as you can present them. That is what Rule Five is all about. The benefits of having clean, clear facts on the table are apparent when it comes time to make a decision. The dangers of making decisions based on tainted information are obvious. You can miss the problem completely if you are not dealing with square facts.

Rule Six:
Define the Objective and Establish
a Plan Before Acting

This one is particular to United, because of its history.

In the command and control era, a boss would walk into a meeting and announce, for example, that the airline would be going to electronic ticketing in six months. Everyone would sit up and respond: "I can do that. I can do my part."

But that wasn't the case, particularly in this example.

Rule Six means we have to define what we are going to accomplish and we have to deliver a real plan for how we are going to accomplish it, or we are going to modify the plan before we even start.

The last vestige of that command and control system at United was when we launched the electronic ticketing project. I happened to walk into one of our reservation centers and some of our reservation people were not yet trained in how to do electronic ticketing.

Travel agents were calling them and asking how travel agents were supposed to do this. They would tell them, "I don't know."

We were losing business. It took sixty days to fix it, and it was a crazy time for everyone.

Rule Seven:
Reach Closure on Decisions

Pretty obvious, isn't it. But it doesn't always happen. Lots of companies, not knowing what to do about a particular issue, will let matters drift by concluding, "We ought to study it more."

I have told my people, "This is not the United Airlines Study Company, this is the United Airlines Decision Company." We try hard to set deadlines. In the interim we gather all the facts we can find. But then we move. There are a lot of managers who have developed this study mode to the level of an art form.

I see that as a version of deceit, sometimes self-deceit.

Rule Eight:
Represent the Team's Decisions As One's Own

Once a team has come to a decision, everyone must support it.

It simply doesn't do to have an icing of consensus that melts away when the project, whatever it happens to be, moves into the field. If a bad mistake is made, or an unanticipated event comes along, fine, regroup. Otherwise, implement.

Rule Nine:
Address a Conflict with a Team Member
Before Mentioning It to Anyone Else

We used to sponsor the Hawaiian Golf Open. We don't do it anymore, but it gave us a good chance to invite a lot of our big customers to Hawaii. One of our customers told John Edwardson (the former president of United) that he had played golf with three of our senior officers and had a unique experience. He didn't hear any of them say anything that was even subtly disparaging of one of the others.

I thought about that story for a while.

A lot of relationships inside a company are soured by unresolved conflicts, and sometimes they come out in a particularly nasty way. I can't tell you how many times in my career I have heard something like this: "Oh, yes, he's a great guy, a great contributor, and he doesn't let his drinking problem get in the way of his work."

Rule Nine says if you have a problem with me, then you should come into my office and we will shut the door and battle it out. We can shout and scream. We can do whatever we want. But we have to resolve the problem. And if we can't, we have to find someone, a facilitator or a referee, to help the two of us sort it out.

It is also aimed at addressing people who avoid conflict.

Avoiding conflict is not healthy in a corporate setting because it lets problems build and fester.

Rule Ten:
Keep My Promises to the Best of My Ability

This one presents an interesting commentary. After a lot of debate and thought, we decided it had to be part of the rules. Of course you should keep your promises. It is just unfortunate that we still feel the need to write that down and post it where everyone can read it.

Rule Eleven:
Establish a Common Agenda
and Mutually Agreed Upon Priorities

We continue to struggle with this issue at United. I wish I could just write down one priority, but it's not that simple. We would be a Johnny One Note company, concentrating on only one objective.

Sometimes there are three or four top priorities that might be in conflict with one another. But the goal is to have a commonly accepted list so everyone is thinking in the same direction. At any given moment, A, B, or C might become more important, depending on circumstances.

The important point is that everyone has to be marching in the same general direction when a challenge presents itself. Creating an agenda and setting priorities helps.

Rule Twelve:
Call a Time-Out When Any of These
Pledges Are Violated

We have some people who are very good at this.

When a meeting is drifting, or when the subject matter has become confusing, someone will call a time-out and ask for clarification. Some folks take this quite literally. It is almost as though they are wearing striped shirts and carrying whistles.

The process seems to work the best among senior employees who understand the concept. They will say, "Wait a minute. I am confused. Could we back up and talk about this some more?"

Like my own early philosophy of working hard to get my bosses promoted, the Rules of the Road are simple to state and difficult to carry out. This is a challenge for the folks who run companies.

The tendency for people at the top is not to show enough patience. Somebody might say, "Wait a minute, I'm confused." But the CEO running the meeting just blows right past them, as though they were not even in the room. That will probably be the last time the CEO hears that person speak up.

I know the problem well because sometimes it's all about me.

We had meetings Mondays at United.

Sometimes, if I had been on the road for a week, collecting experiences, I would go to those sessions all pent up and full of ideas. If I allowed it to happen, I became impatient and I would start barking. My colleagues at the meeting would actually recoil.

By the end of the meeting, I would have to apologize for my behavior.

Some of my colleagues then told me I was misreading the moment, that I was really just reflecting my passion for the work. But I asked them not to tell me that because I knew I was breaking a rule.

It is very easy for a CEO to slip into that role. After all, he has been appointed king. But what that really means is that he doesn't have to throw his weight around. People already know his power.

If you are going to embrace these rules, then, they must be taken seriously.

Sometimes, the lesson learning has to start right at the top.

ELEVEN

★

Golden Years

I have flunked retirement three times.

It has been one of my greatest failures.

I am not alone in facing this struggle, a common problem that affects aggressive and healthy people at every level. We Type A's have spent the last half of the century trying to convince everyone that life is work.

Then, somewhere in the mid-1980s, probably because of short-term thinking, top managers started inviting middle-aged middle managers to leave the workplace in great numbers. It became an accepted management practice. Call it right-sizing, downsizing, outsizing, whatever coating you want for layoffs and shrinking.

It was a mistake.

Take a close look at businesses today and you will find many of those companies in such a struggle to find experienced employees that they are calling their former workers back to their jobs, sometimes at a lot more money. That is a sign that at least some businesses now recognize what they lost.

Long after making money was an important part of the agenda for me, I continued to work. I jog a lot and recently ran a marathon. I am not tired, worn out, or run-down. I can outlast, or at least keep up with, people half my age. I have always defined my life by the business mountains I could climb.

There are plenty of others like me. In early 1999, I spent months talking to other executives, some of them retired, trying to learn how to succeed at giving up going to work every day. Many of them told me exactly the same thing. I had to learn how to retire the same way I learned how to work. It doesn't happen automatically.

I believe it is time to challenge some of the assumptions about working life. For me, that has meant a retirement that isn't really a retirement in the traditional sense. I get to spend a lot more time with my family in Aspen now, which is important to me. But I am also working with an investment capital group and doing several humanitarian projects.

I am expanding my experience and sharing my experiences at the same time.

The simple lesson I want to emphasize is that experience matters.

To my mind, in measuring experience against short-term costs, it is the experience that carries the value.

I know that, and have known it for years, because of Teflon-coated ball joints!

The auto industry has been using Teflon-coated ball joints in cars for years. The Teflon makes them maintenance-free. I know this because I was there, as they say, at the creation of the Teflon-coated ball joint.

This is a story worth telling because of what it says about the value of experience.

I didn't know anyone, or much of anything about cars, when I joined Ford Motor Co. in 1957. I was moving into Ford's Edsel division. I thought that would be a great start, even though I really wanted to be in labor relations. Instead, I was hired to handle salary and personnel records.

The whole division collapsed within three months of the day I arrived.

I didn't do it!

The problem was that the Edsel, with its push-button gear shifter in the center of the steering column and its radical design, ran head-on into the recession of 1958. People wanted lower-priced cars. The Edsel was expensive, didn't work well, and in some eyes, was as ugly as a bridge troll.

I recall thinking, "Man, how can I do so bad so quick?" I literally lived one of those "And when you leave, turn out the lights" experiences. It was every man for himself in those days.

I thought I would just pack all my worldly possessions in the trunk of my car and go back to St. Louis to hang out with my parents and send out some résumés.

I was on my way out the door of Ford when I got a call that one of my interviews had clicked. I was sent off to a new assignment, administrative assistant to the chief engineer. His job was to create what would become the Ford Falcon.

My assignment was to take care of everything that had nothing to do with engineering. Get the drafting tables. Hire new people. But as part of this assignment, I sat in on all the engineering meetings. It was a terrific education, because I got to learn all about cars.

I met a man who was experience come to life. If you are lucky, you meet people like him all the time in business. They are the employees who know how to make things work, how to get things done, right and on time.

There were eighty engineers in the Falcon group, but there was only one man who could lock himself in a room and come out two weeks later to present the complete design of an automobile. Nobody else, including the chief engineer, knew that much about cars and the interrelationships of the parts of an automobile.

This man was golden within the group because of all that experience. He didn't just walk into Ford with that kind of knowledge, he built it over a long career. He was then in his late sixties, working part-time after his retirement.

There were engineers in the group who were experts on suspension. Experts on windshields. Experts on seats. Experts in all manner of specialized tasks. But he was the only one who was expert at full automobile design.

These people were completely passionate about designing cars.

The challenge of the Falcon was to design an automobile that would represent big breakthroughs, including reduced scheduled maintenance. And until then, maintenance was what ball joints were all about. They had to be lubricated frequently and closely watched, because once they dried out, they wore down quickly.

What is a ball joint? You have a lot of similar devices spread all over your body. Anything that goes up and down or turns on a car needs that kind of a joint, and the front wheels need them most of all. The ball joint, combined with shock absorbers, lets the tire bounce on the road; it gives the car some flexibility. It's one of those pieces of equipment that get little notice until something goes wrong. When ball joints fail, havoc ensues. The front of the car can hit the ground. If that happens at any speed, look out.

We came up with a design for Teflon-coated ball joints. In those days, it was space-age and practical. If we made it work, the need to have those joints greased and cared for, at the driver's expense, would disappear. The big test came Christmas Eve.

It did not go well.

The chief engineer got the call first. We had three or four cars in tests with the new ball joints and two of them failed. They weren't just little failures. The Teflon-coated joints split apart on the test tracks. It was a bonding problem with the Teflon. The front ends of the cars dropped and there were sparks and pieces of metal everywhere.

That presented a huge challenge. We were on a tight design schedule to get the car into production. The fix couldn't wait until the holidays were over.

These engineers weren't grumbling about having to work on Christmas Eve, but the failure was almost like losing a member of a family.

They were veterans and they knew what they were doing and they just didn't stop until they had the problem solved. It took two days to redesign to conventional, non-Teflon parts so as not to miss the targeted deadlines. I was impressed by that performance because it taught me the value of filling vacuums. Companies do not run, for the most part, on procedures, systems, and manuals. Really good employees fill in vacuums.

You just jump in and do whatever needs to be done.

They didn't care about boundaries or turf. They just wanted to solve the problem. It was the mix of passion and experience that was so exhilarating.

Watching that kind of experience at work really opened my eyes and taught me a lesson about where value really resides in a company. I saw the same level of experience at work when the Ford engineers got a chance to take a first look at one of Chevrolet's new models, the Corvair.

In those days, there was a reciprocal swap of new pre-production cars among the manufacturers.

The first time a car came off a production line, you would give a couple of them to your competitors and they would give you a couple of their new models for testing.

We ran a handling test on the track. The cars were a Plymouth Valiant, a Ford Falcon, and a Chevrolet Corvair. I will never forget watching some of the films with the engineers. One of those cantankerous old Ford engineers was sitting beside me eyeing the Corvair test. He pulls my sleeve and says, "Look at how that car fishtails. That's really bad."

His experienced eye focused on a flaw that would ultimately kill the Corvair and open a loud and passionate national debate on auto design safety, spearheaded by Ralph Nader. But that Ford veteran saw the Corvair problem and knew intuitively that under certain conditions, the car had trouble.

I wonder what Ford would have done if it had just

squeezed its veterans off the scene to bring in lower-cost, inexperienced engineers?

The message is as clear today as it was forty years ago.

Don't chase experienced people out. Don't tempt them out. Keep them! Over time, you will have more people working with you who are age fifty than age thirty. That is not only okay, it is quite good. That is where your market is heading, and those are the people who will know best how to cater to that market.

The challenge employers face is to adapt successfully to recognize these kinds of changes.

It is as important to be aware of this change inside the company as it is to be aware of it in the marketplace.

I had an experience at Chrysler that was an early example of responding to the aging of the workforce. We had one of our oldest assembly plants in the center of Detroit. It was in one of the toughest parts of town, but we made a decision that we wanted to keep that plant open. It was good for business and it was good for the community because it provided so many jobs in an area that was rapidly losing hope.

Over the years, the workforce at that plant had dropped from nine thousand to about four thousand, and the average age of the workers was forty-eight. At the time, that was an advanced age for industrial workers. Many of them had been hired in the 1960s at a period of almost full employment. Just about anybody who walked in could get hired. Very few had much of an education.

There was a challenge from the marketplace, too. Chrysler was in trouble with consumers because of quality problems. We wanted to address quality along with the issue of the age of our workers.

Instead of closing that plant down, we decided to invest. We wanted to make it an easier place to work, expecting better quality in return.

But that wasn't a simple challenge.

Historically, the car bodies moved down long assembly

lines. The people who were assigned to install doors would have to bend down to do their work. Other workers on the line had to crawl inside the vehicles and twist themselves around to complete their operations.

We redesigned the plant so that the car bodies actually lifted or turned to the most convenient position for the teams working on specific tasks.

It worked. We built good-quality Jeeps, and we transformed the workplace to meet the needs of an aging workforce before other factories started using the same approach. Work became easier and our trained and experienced workforce stayed in place. Imagine what it would have cost to move the operation elsewhere and hire and train new employees.

Those folks had great value to Chrysler, but we had to work hard to find a way to continue using it.

These stories bring an old saying about experience to mind. In a room full of people who only know how to wear loafers, the character who can still tie his shoes has a great advantage.

You don't want to shed the people who still know how to tie their shoes.

When you push years of practical experience out the door, value walks out with it. I know that flies directly in the face of a lot of modern managerial thinking. But my attitude comes from four decades of experience. I know what it is to cut deeply to save a company.

But there is another element wrapped inside this question of aging that I also want to address, and it has lessons that apply to everyone from the corporate suite to line operators.

We all must change attitudes toward retirement and that means changing attitudes toward work and its meaning in life, and changing attitudes of management toward experienced workers.

I think I am a classic example of one of those weaknesses of American management. Our work has become our identity. Our company is part of our family. There is a parallel in the lives of many women, particularly those who stay home to raise children. The home, the family, defines them. They face a sea change, too, when the children grow up and move away.

If your work is your identity and you don't have any more work to do, then you are lost. It is the dark side of loving your work. It becomes a trap when the time for retirement arrives. But the loss stretches beyond the personal; your company loses you, too, and all the value you brought to the workplace over the years.

Give me half a chance and I will bore my dinner partner about my work. I try to get interested in other attractions, going to a museum, for example. But after forty-five minutes, my mind clicks over to Monday's business problems.

This has the earmarks of a successful career.

But what does it say about how people in business live their lives and develop their values? This problem—work as life—extends far beyond the executive suite, to middle managers and, frequently, to workers.

Why is it a problem?

Well, people don't stop developing at the midpoint in their lives. During this process of failing at retirement, I continued to grow with every new experience. I continued adding to my own value.

I am not bragging. It happens to almost everyone who continues to work. Under the proper conditions, each day on the job gives them the equivalent of a day of graduate school business education.

That creates tremendous value.

Knowledge is a difficult asset to measure. But I wonder how many millions of dollars of value walk out the door every day because American business culture is so obsessed with youth that it thinks little of pushing its veterans out.

Paying attention to youth is not bad in itself, of course.

Hiring for the future is one of the most important challenges in the modern workplace. You want to collect the best battalions of employees, train them better than workers have ever been trained before, and free them so they make good, productive decisions.

But the new hires don't learn everything they need to know in the first three weeks, or even the first three years, on the job. The ideal is to have a good mix. A company needs mentors as much as it needs aggressive, smart young people.

I think back over my own experiences, first at Ford and Chrysler, and then to investment banking, real estate management, and, finally, United Airlines.

I didn't walk into any of those jobs as a completed package. My experience had taught me how to learn what I needed to do quickly, and it taught me the value of turning to veterans for the kind of knowledge I needed. I don't know what I would have become if those veterans had not been willing to share their knowledge with me.

My thoughts drift back to situations I have seen many times.

A new employee will have memorized everything there is to know about the rule book, will have completed all of the training sessions, and will be better prepared than any worker in the past to handle the challenges of the job.

Then the inevitable occurs.

Something happens that is not in the book.

Picture the new employee in that situation. A disaster is at hand and there is no road map available to negotiate safely through the situation.

Standing just to the side of this young employee is a veteran who has been on the job for twenty-five, maybe thirty years. He has seen disasters come and go and has learned so well the lesson of thinking on his feet that it has become second nature. The new worker turns to this veteran, presents the problem, and receives a suggestion, based on experience, about how to proceed.

At the beginning of the twentieth century, people generally lived, perhaps, into their fifties and would be worn out by the hard physical labor that defined their lives. The miners would be used up. The factory workers would not be able to handle the physical challenge of the job. The salesclerks who spent so many years standing up would lose their legs and that sense of courtesy and humor so important in dealing with customers.

Moving quickly and working with your muscles was the formula for survival, if not success, in the industrial era.

Guess what?

We don't live in an industrial era anymore. Most people work with their brains these days, not with their backs. The assumption that people wear out in middle age is very much a part of nineteenth- and early-twentieth-century thinking. If you embrace that old value, you are ignoring reality and damaging your company in the process.

Think of experience, then, as mental weight lifting.

Because of advances in medicine and much more attention paid to quality of life, we have added about three decades to our lifespan during the past century. I listened to a scientist talk about this extension of lifespan.

The conventional thought is that we have added years to the end of life. But this scientist believes those years were not tacked on at the end, they were inserted somewhere in the middle. This change expanded healthy middle age; it did not extend what we view as old age.

People have changed. Work has changed. Now it is time for attitudes toward retirement to change, too.

All kinds of assumptions about the needs and abilities of an aging society must change, too. The federal government has developed an obsession about Social Security. But what role will Social Security play in a healthy, aging society that decides it just wants to keep working?

That doesn't mean everyone will be punching the time clock and putting in forty hours a week. But it is likely that people will come to craft their own definitions of work as time passes. Maybe they will be working efficiently for twenty hours a week, or maybe their work will carry a different value. Their contributions won't be measured in terms of hours at work. They will be measured in terms of the value they bring to the workplace.

But how long is it going to take for managers to recognize that and to change their own values?

Think about what this transformation means for our society.

The most important message is that productivity doesn't end somewhere in the fifth or sixth decade. Take a look at all the people who were pushed out in their mid-fifties only a few years ago and measure what they are doing now. Some are teachers, college students, independent business consultants, or employees at other companies.

They walk in the door with knowledge and self-confidence stamped all over them, unless, however, they have had the door slammed in their face once too often with the hidden message "You're too old."

The significance of this big change, the aging of society, doesn't stop at corporate attitudes toward older workers. Demographic shifts are already having a huge impact on the marketplace.

It may have been suitable to aim marketing messages at the baby-boom generation as it was growing up. Now it is time to recognize that the baby boomers are growing old, but not the way their parents and grandparents grew old. Many of them have spent their lives on brainwork, adding value as they added experience. They are also moving through middle age with strong incomes and assets, which makes them an ideal target market.

Their lives will certainly be changing, but they will not be sedentary. When we watched U.S. Senator John Glenn's return to space on the shuttle, it should have represented a wake-up call for marketers. The senator was giving people in their fifties, sixties, and even seventies permission and an endorsement to have active, productive lives in the workplace, as consumers, and in society.

They are healthier, better educated, and wealthier than

any generation in history, and they are not about to move quietly into a passive retirement.

It pays for the business world to recognize that message, too.

How?

First, take a look at the numbers.

The U.S. Bureau of the Census, font of statistics, projects population into what seems to be an eternity of charts, but the numbers tell an important story.

Last year, those census figures showed, only 15 percent of the U.S. population was between the ages of sixty and eighty-four years old. But that group will become 20 percent of the population by 2020, an increase of 33 percent in size, which is huge growth in a potential market segment.

Going a little deeper into the numbers, only 26 percent of the population was age fifty or older a few years ago, but the Census Bureau projects that 35 percent of the population will be over fifty years old by 2020. It estimates that some 235,000 Americans will be over one hundred years old!

Other surveys present even more revealing conclusions about the attitudes in this oldest part of the U.S. population.

If you look at today's baby boomers, those currently between the ages of thirty-five and fifty-four, a full 74 percent told Scudder Kemper Investments that they planned to do some kind of paid work in retirement. But the attitude isn't limited to the boomer generation.

Some 54 percent of those in what is called the "Swing Generation," between the ages of fifty-three and sixty-five expect to be earning some money in retirement, as do 34 percent of those who are currently in the "World War II" generation, ages sixty-six and older.

Even 68 percent of those young Generation Xers, now between ages twenty-two and thirty-three, plan to be working for dollars after retirement age.

Right now, about 12 percent of all Americans over age sixty-five are in the labor force, some 3.8 million people. If the other projections hold true, that number and the income it creates will be climbing dramatically as time passes.

Given these projections, it's time for an attitude change.

My first piece of advice for business leaders is to get some experts to look at the changing demographics of consumers. Where is your audience now and where is it going? I think these specialists will find that the target is shifting northward, even as those census projections shift northward.

That being the case, it is important to move away from one of those simplistic adages that was so dominant, for example, in the car industry: You can sell old people young people's cars, but you can't sell young people old people's cars.

Stop addressing only young people.

If selling is your business—cars for example—you must be aware that the biggest chunk of the nation's population has advanced beyond sports cars that are a little scary and difficult to sit in.

That doesn't mean they don't want sporty cars.

It does mean they want sporty cars that are a lot more comfortable than the models available just a few years ago. Getting in and getting out becomes an issue for people who are getting older.

The primary market might be a lot more interested in safe, fast, comfortable sedans with speedometers with bigger numbers to read, something that gives people a taste of the sensation they had when life was all about the small fast cars, intense romance, and the stimulating days of youth.

It's just that they might want to cut the risks a bit.

If those who are aging still wanted Cadillacs the size of ocean liners, the market for spunky Mercedes-Benzes, BMWs, and snappy Lexuses would not be so vibrant.

That may be why those big, fast SUVs have leather

bucket seats, gigantic V-8 engines, and instrument panels that look like they come from F-16s.

We obviously live in a culture that has been in love with denim for decades, but tight jeans are the wrong products for an aging society. That's why the new range of jeans options now includes the kindly description: "relaxed fit."

It won't pay to think of youth as the ultimate target market for a whole range of products that are becoming the favorites of the boomers as they age. Sailboats, running shoes, exercise equipment, expensive bicycles (but with well-cushioned seats), in-line skates, cross-country skis, cell phones, these are all products that seem inherently youthful, but are becoming must-haves for a lot of people who are no longer young.

America Online looked at its subscriber base and found the average age was forty. These are people who first got comfortable with computers at work, and carried that habit home with them. And if the average user age is forty, that means there are a lot of fifty- and sixty-year-olds hearing "You've Got Mail!" too!

This is what happens when there is a confluence of disposable income and disposable time, and those are two of the important earmarks of a prosperous chunk of population that is heading into what used to be known as quiet old age.

If you are providing services, the same message applies.

Tastes shift as the population ages.

Airlines are not pouring as much hard liquor as they used to. It pays to recognize the fact that a big part of the population likes bottled water. And if it has a thirst for beer, it might want only one and it might want the brand to be fairly exotic.

Business needs to shift emphasis to that demographic center and understand what that body of consumers really wants and needs.

It's no longer safe to assume everyone will be scrambling to make airport connections, for example. As the population ages, a different set of services comes into play. Airlines have to account for the fact that more and more people are going to be needing help getting from point A to point B. If they are accommodated by making that journey a little easier, then they will continue to travel. The airlines that handle the needs of these folks will get their business.

That is why more and more convenience carts, wheelchairs, and jitneys are showing up at big airports. I suspect we will see the day when those long aisles at O'Hare in Chicago or the vast corridors at Atlanta yield to special-use lanes that are provided solely for people who can't dash from plane to plane. Look for more elevators, too.

Those television monitors that announce arrivals and departures are going to have to be in larger type, too. We are already finding ways to eliminate that long wait in line at the ticket counter, for many reasons, but one is to make travel easier for older people.

Older folks refuse to spend a long time standing in line.

My concerns about management attitudes toward aging don't stop with the workforce and the marketplace. I see these problems playing out in boardrooms, too. It's not prudent to chase so many valuable people off boards simply because of age.

Paul Volcker, former chairman of the Federal Reserve, once described as the second most powerful person in the world, next to the president, had to leave the United board at age seventy last year, and United is missing his experience.

I think about artists in this context.

What if someone had asked Picasso why he kept painting even though he had become a tremendously successful man? I don't think anyone would ever ask that kind of a question about an artist. But they ask it of people who have become wealthy at business all the time.

The challenge, then, is to think of business veterans the same way we think of artists. They have a contribution to make, they continue to love their work, and they are vastly experienced.

I find it strange that our society continues to hold out this carrot: Work very hard and you won't have to work anymore. The reward for very hard work and success is that you don't have to work anymore. Pick up any travel magazine or turn on the television and you see this message everywhere. The image is that you have worked hard and now you get to spend your time on the beach.

But when you get to that beach, it isn't so wonderful.

On the personal side, I know what happens when you leave the workplace before your time, heading for the beach, or in my case, for the ski slopes. This experience is common to a lot of modern executives.

My first attempt at retirement came well after we had turned Chrysler around.

Was I able to settle into my plan for retirement?

No.

I was as nervous as a cat. I was emotionally unsettled. Somebody could have called up and said, "Mr. Greenwald, would you like to come and talk to us about being the chief executive officer of our corner grocery store?" I would have rushed off to New York for the interview.

I was overenergized. If I had fifteen minutes in a day that wasn't planned, I got twitchy. If the phone wasn't ringing, I got twitchy. If I thought a week was coming with nothing to do, I would go to interview for just about anything. I would do anything but sit still.

I needed action.

I suppose a psychologist would say that I needed to be wanted. I still don't know what the exact problem was, but I knew that I would not be able to carry out my plan. I had flunked retirement. I simply could not enjoy what I had.

Other CEOs tell me the best way to succeed at retirement is to be selective about the calls you receive and the opportunities you pursue.

I want to live where I want to live, not where I work. I am

also intrigued by the thought of making my family my business. I am drawn to the challenge of helping children who are at economic risk. I am most interested in public service work, and I am already involved in a capital investment partnership, where I can help smaller companies.

I must honestly say that I don't know where it will all lead.

But I do know that I am a walking, working example of the generation that created me. We are full of experience and full of energy. I doubt my retirement will lead to a rocking chair soon.

None of us is really done with our work, yet.

TWELVE

★

Who Killed Loyalty?

America's companies spent decades building up employee loyalty, then crushed it over a few short years.

Now we are paying the price.

In the world of the Internet start-up, where countless thousands of young workers are beginning new careers, loyalty is in short supply.

It has been replaced by the siren call of stock options.

The pay might be low, but the options, should a company succeed, offer the promise of a fortune. Everyone in the business world seems to have stories of the 15 cents option that became the $100 a share stock.

This has created a major turnover, even churning, of the techies and content providers so crucial to successful companies.

The message in this new world might be: "If you want loyalty, buy a dog. People work for money."

In that other world so familiar to the workers of the last century, loyalty has been chased away by an era of ruthless cost and job cutting that shattered the old unwritten contract: Work hard and you have a job for life.

Consider these new realities.

A successful start-up like Yahoo! can create overnight millionaires, while the other companies, Sears, IBM, Hershey Foods among them, compete for fewer and fewer qualified job candidates. They no longer offer the security

that was such a powerful magnet. If their executives hold
stock options, they disappear and hunt for more promising
positions if the company's stock drops and their options
become worthless.

This is creating a huge challenge for the industrial companies, for large companies everywhere, and even for law
firms and management consulting companies, which once
had the advantage in the employment contest because they
could offer the promise of partnerships with fat payoffs
after appropriate on-the-job dues were paid.

Why spend ten years building to a partnership position when you can ride stock options to a fortune almost
overnight by taking a key position with a hot company?

There is no doubt about the depth of this problem.

Newspaper help-wanted ads in some markets, which
used to suffer during recessions as companies cut back on
advertising budgets for hiring, are declining because it
does little good to advertise a job for which there is no
available worker.

Could the rebirth of loyalty be one of the solutions to
the shortage of workers?

You remember loyalty, don't you?

Put simply, employers developed a sense of trust in their
workers, and workers developed a sense of trust in their
employers.

I've thought a lot about loyalty over four decades.

I have seen the relationship between workers and top
management change, with the final, wrenching separation
occurring in the mid-1980s between the people at the top
of companies and the people who work for companies.

There is an easy way to understand where loyalty went.

The folks who came along before us used it all up.

That problem didn't begin and end in corporate America. It certainly wasn't caused by the development of the Internet.

The only good news to come out of this change is that,

as a nation, we are more a country of individuals than we were before it began. Individuals tend to question things more. They are less inclined to follow foolish, dumb, or bad radical ideas of others.

But where did loyalty go?

Somehow over the past century, we persuaded ourselves that it was okay to lay off factory workers.

Looking back, I don't think that was ever really okay, but the factory workers came to accept it and crafted their lives around the assumption that they might lose their jobs for a time if the economy soured or a business got in trouble.

But the more significant change came the day we decided it was okay to lay off white-collar workers.

That was the day loyalty marched out the door.

I have heard all the reasons and plenty of excuses.

I'm in the middle of restructuring. I couldn't help it. It wasn't my fault there was a downturn in the economy.

Many are just that, excuses. Did you really have to restructure? What was the goal? When the economy went sour, did you turn to layoffs first, or were they a last resort that was necessary to save your company? Or were you trying to improve a bottom line that was reasonably healthy, using the economic downturn as cover?

There are many circumstances beyond a CEO's control that might require layoffs and restructuring of a company. But what bothers me the most about the reengineering and restructuring fads at the end of the last century was that we made such champions of CEOs who played hardball and slashed employment. Layoffs should always have been the last option on the list, not the first.

There is no doubt that reengineering their products added value to some companies and made them much more efficient. But in many other cases, those projects were not aimed at improving efficiency. They were aimed at the short-term bottom line, and aimed there without much sense of the true ongoing cost of deep employment cuts.

We have made heroes out of corporate slashers when we

really should have been looking at the process a lot more critically, recognizing that there are better ways to handle the problem than layoffs. A lot of those CEOs could have used attrition and buyouts to cut the size of the workforce. Instead, they opted for deep cuts.

We should have been criticizing them for undermining the last loyalties in their own companies.

Loyalty was an asset, which they ignored and then destroyed.

They also created a false model of prosperity in which cost cutting was the pathway to profits, and that can only work for a short time.

The great danger is that if you embrace cost cutting to enhance profits, you are looking at costs instead of growth, and growth is the only viable way to guarantee profits and stability for the long term.

The other factor in the decline of loyalty is bigness.

I have always wanted to duplicate some specific examples I have seen in every company I have worked for.

Remember the story about the collapsing Teflon ball joints at Ford on Christmas Eve? You could argue that it was the inventiveness of the engineering team that solved that problem. But I think it was their dedication to the task, their loyalty to one another, their sense that they had an objective to meet for their company that really led to the solution.

Even in my last job, if I went into one of our United Airlines cities where we had a hundred workers, I usually found a team with a can-do attitude. They all helped each other. They all cared about each other. They all cared about the company.

I recall a visit to Oklahoma, where I found one of our United employees who was five months pregnant. She told me, "Oh, it's that time of year again, I have to retrain on how to run the cherry picker."

That is the de-icing machine. It is a piece of equipment that has a long arm with a bucket on the end. It might seem pretty daunting to retrain yourself in de-icing when you are five months pregnant. But that was what was on this woman's mind.

There is real economy in an operation that small.

You seldom find that kind of dedication or those relationships where there are five thousand employees in the operation.

In those cases, people tend to think, "This is my job. Leave me alone. I will do it myself." Teamwork is harder to come by.

Take a simple lesson from that experience.

Even if you have 15,000 employees, or in the case of United, 100,000 employees, your company will function a lot better if people think of themselves as important parts of smaller units.

It does little good to think of yourself as one of 100,000 nameless characters at Megacorp, Inc., complete with a company ID and a number, say ID No. 94,023. But if you can help convince an employee that he or she is part of a small group playing an important role in a much larger machine, the outcome will be different.

Studies show what Stephen Ambrose has conveyed so brilliantly in his war histories. Soldiers don't think of themselves—and risk their lives—as part of a huge army; they do that for people they know who deserve their trust and loyalty, people who depend on them, commonly a group no larger than an infantry squad.

No matter how big your company is, find ways to structure work so that people are in smaller groups, so that they can know and depend on one another.

I know the argument.

Several smaller groups cost more in supervision. It is easy to quantify that cost. You need faith to believe small groups will give you net better productivity, but they will.

It takes faith to believe investing in loyalty will pay off.

The results of a successful effort to rebuild loyalty will be apparent. Sick days will decline in number. Workmen's

Compensation cases will go down. Labor troubles will still be there, but the goal on both sides will be to solve them, not to use them as an excuse to fight.

I am proud to say that in surveys, 80 percent of United employees planned to stay at United for their full careers.

Who can blame workers for abandoning loyalty?

Maybe that is why the question of loyalty is so important to me.

I was that young person who started out with an assumption about hard work, honesty, and loyalty.

Later, in my darkest, most selfish ambitious moments, I never wanted to be called "Chainsaw Jerry" or "Machine Gun Greenwald" and it upsets me that that kind of performance was so richly rewarded and firmly embraced.

I thought that era was terrible. It was the point at which the undermining of loyalty shifted into high gear.

If you lay off two people in a work group of ten, those who stay at work will abandon any sense of loyalty they had. They may be next. Loyalty is no longer in their interest. They are certainly going to show signs on the surface of working harder, but it is likely that their résumés are out.

If a call comes from a headhunter, they are more likely to return it.

Some modern business "heroes" don't seem to care much about that.

If you think of employees as targets of long-term investment (and a good company invests in their education, their experience, their performance), then these investments walk straight out the door whenever those employees leave.

A lot of critics of the era of reengineering point to the Japanese and argue that they did very well without laying off employees.

But I don't think that is the right model, either.

The Japanese created artificial employment, and that is bad. When their economic conditions went soft, they couldn't keep it up and the whole process unraveled on them. They had to let go of people who never had real jobs in the first place.

It's wrong to find work for people that isn't real work.

I recognize there are times when corporations need to reduce employment, either because they made mistakes internally, or because the external situation changes.

I have a three-step plan for handling that problem.

Number One: Use attrition. When people retire, quit, or die, don't replace them.

Number Two: If attrition doesn't work, offer tempting buyouts.

Number Three: Only in desperation, when you are running out of cash and it looks like your company might die, should you craft a layoff plan.

But even at that stage, first lay off a proportionate number of people in top management. Everyone in your company must know that the pain created by the economic trouble is shared across the board.

You have to remember that no matter how difficult the challenge is today, there is always tomorrow, and you don't want to face it with an embittered workforce.

If you truly care about loyalty, there are two other issues you should be very careful about.

You cannot have a 20 percent, or 50 percent, or 100 percent increase in pay for the chief executive officer while you are laying people off. The gap between executive salaries and compensation for workers is already too wide. Making it even wider during layoffs is a formula for revolution that puts a dagger straight into the heart of any loyalty that might remain at your company.

The second action you should never take is to embrace a layoff plan when your company is making a good profit.

People aren't stupid.

It is a powerful signal that tells everyone near-term profit improvement is all that matters to you.

People want assurances that hard work will be rewarded

with good pay and long-term stability. They can help handle hard times if they can safely assume everyone is working toward the same end.

But there is no quicker way to crush that attitude than to send out pink slips as a quick solution to economic trouble, or as a dash to trade a company's long-term health for short-term gain.

Communicate honestly, candidly, and often.

Be the first to sacrifice. Be a visionary leader. If you tell people, "Look, follow me and we will succeed," and they follow you for a while and you do succeed, then you will be rebuilding loyalty.

Accept that you can do this a hundred times successfully, but if you fail on the 101st attempt, loyalty will decline. This is a long, long rebuilding process. Today, there is very little tolerance for senior management mistakes. There has been too much history of the wrong kind.

A CEO creates the environment that surrounds his company, and environment plays an important role in rebuilding loyalty.

When I arrived at United, I went searching for advice on how to repair a mood that had been poisoned over years of bitter struggle between labor and management. There was suspicion everywhere. The top managers were hiding from the workers, and the workers were certainly hiding from management.

That is no way to run an employee-owned company. With employee ownership, everyone becomes a worker and everyone becomes a manager, even though the job titles and salaries don't show it. The goals and needs converge.

To my surprise, I learned that small gestures from a CEO most certainly do count.

Every time you get on a United plane, I was told, stop to talk to the people at the gate, introduce yourself to the flight attendants and the pilots. Spend some time talking to them.

I have done that ever since. I found that I enjoyed it, and I suspect the people I talked to enjoyed it, too. If that sounds to you like the company king is out slumming, then that is a measure of how far you have been carried from the interests of your employees.

A good CEO at the very least takes mental notes during these visits. If a complaint comes up that seems to have merit, he is presented with a golden opportunity to build trust by finding some way to address it as quickly as possible. No matter how hard a CEO tries, there are no informal conversations with workers. The workers are sending messages and the CEO is obliged, in many cases, to respond.

I have already mentioned the danger of using the phrase "trust me."

People don't want to hear "trust me."

I always tried to make a point of telling folks I was not asking them for their trust. I was asking them to watch how I do my job and to judge me that way. It is unfortunate that that phrase, "trust me," has lost its value.

Performance is its replacement.

Sometimes over the past few years in my down moments I have wondered whether rebuilding loyalty is even possible.

Maybe we should simply conclude that loyalty is like a lot of other things in the human endeavor, something that is gone now. I have put myself in check on this issue many times, thinking that perhaps I am one of those people looking for something that just doesn't exist anymore.

My Aspen joke comes to mind. It comes from folks who remember the old Aspen of hippies and cowboys with great fondness.

How many Aspenites does it take to change a light bulb?

One to unscrew the bad one. One to screw in the new one. A third to sit and look at the old light bulb and the new light bulb and talk about how the old light bulb was really a lot nicer than the new light bulb.

But I don't think this is just me in search of something we once had.

I think if you talked to older folks about the issue, they would understand the value of loyalty right away. They would see it as a most important part of the relationship between managers and workers and they would want to get it back.

But if you asked the same kinds of questions to people who are thirty, they would say, "Well, do you want the buggy whip back, too?"

They are planning their lives in full recognition that what matters is themselves, and finding a way to succeed on their own terms.

I think that is admirable in some ways.

But I also think it is a mistake.

I have already declared myself as being on the front lines in the struggle to get loyalty back. It certainly can't hurt, and if it succeeds, I believe it can be enormously effective.

My belief is that people who trust and like to work with each other are going to deliver a better service or a better product than those who don't.

This road, the loyalty road, is a tough one to walk.

The odds are not in a CEO's favor these days. When I look around corporate America as to which companies have it and which don't, I know that it isn't always the CEO's fault that loyalty has declined.

One of the success models that impresses me the most is Southwest Airlines. Herb Kelleher started with a small group of people, which helps. Start-up companies have a better shot at building, then retaining loyalty even though they are basically running from the wolf for the first few years and struggling to survive.

Herb Kelleher started early, had a business concept that he refined early on, and he has been very successful. He

runs a company that has continued to grow for more than
two decades without layoffs.

I have never talked about loyalty to the people who run
Nucor, the steel company, but they also started from
scratch. I'm told they have an interesting philosophy toward work. If there is only four days' worth of work in a
given week, then everyone from top to bottom only works
four days. And they only get paid, from top to bottom, for
four days of work.

Fred Smith started Federal Express.

He started out with a handful of pilots and an extraordinary idea and now it has become this really big and very
successful company. But the pilots have decided they don't
want to depend just on Fred Smith, so Fred and the pilots
are at it. I think most of the employees are on Fred's side
in this conflict, but the struggle is creating a tension that
could put a crack in loyalty at Federal Express.

My guess is that if you looked at the hundred most admired companies, you would find relatively stronger loyalty
than in most of the companies that didn't make the list.
But the fact remains that most companies in America don't
have loyalty anymore.

Do they even realize that?

There are some pretty direct ways of finding out.

First, don't ask your officers.

They are not likely to tell you, "Gee, everyone hates us"
or "They think we are money-grubbing liars," because they
know the next question will be "Why?"

And that carries them into territory they don't want to
visit.

The answers might be, "Because our behavior over the
past decade has been hateful from the workers' perspective" or, worse, "Because we earned this distrust."

Go to a third party and contract for an employee attitude survey.

The results will hit you right between the eyes, I am certain.

Ask one simple question: Do you trust senior management when it tells you something?

What if only 25 percent of your employees believe you?

A CEO must be more than just tangentially conscious of the fact that he is gambling with people's jobs. He cannot stop with the thought: "I am going to hire some new people. They don't have jobs now and if my new plan doesn't work, they won't have jobs then, either."

Once inside the company, new employees are going to expect to be treated just like the other employees.

Why should these new employees be as committed as everyone else if they are not really working under the same terms? Why should they make that trade-off, that loyalty exchange, when they know the company is offering no loyalty on its side of the formula?

Because of that, a CEO must be cautious about implementing growth or acquisition plans. If he is selling off a part of his company, he must do his best to be sure that the people move with the sale to the new company.

It occurs to me that, on questions of job security, the needs of employees are a lot more like the needs of lenders of a company than the needs of shareholders. The shareholders would urge management to take risks, because if the gamble pays off, the stock price goes up.

But a creditor would urge caution, knowing that if a gamble doesn't work out, his loans won't be repaid. An employee doesn't want his job to be part of a corporate gamble.

The grapevine is a terrible way for an employee to learn that a company has a plan under way that might cost a job. A CEO's first goal should be to make certain the employees know what is going on before they read about it in the newspaper.

If a CEO can't do that because of the confidential nature of a negotiation, then it has to be made certain afterward that the employees know why they couldn't be told about it at the time.

"I was right in the middle of a merger, and if I had told you all about it, it would have wrecked the deal."

Know in the beginning that if a survey is taken ten years hence, and employees are asked whether management communicates well, the answer will always be no. Even facing that reality, the CEO who communicates clearly and frequently about what is happening inside the business will be a lot better off, in terms of loyalty, than the CEO who is not forthcoming.

We have some lessons to learn from our counterparts around the world. As businesses consolidate and buy one another across national boundaries, the danger is that this American disloyalty disease will take hold elsewhere, when just the opposite should be happening. We should be learning about loyalty from them.

European and Asian managers don't think the way American managers think on this subject. In some countries, the government strongly discourages laying off workers. When a company is in trouble it has to search for more creative, productive solutions to reduce employment.

I have hope that as business becomes truly global, American companies may find themselves compromising more on the question of job cutbacks. I am not proposing the regulatory rigidity of Europe that prevents employment reductions when they are needed, but I am suggesting more care of people planning—some of the elements of which are found in Europe and Asia.

Looking back over my five years at United, I have realized that one of my assumptions about loyalty—that employee ownership alone would quickly translate into an increase in company loyalty—was wrong. United employees want job security. They want good pay. They want their stock to rise. A healthy company can meet all three of those needs, but employee ownership alone won't do it.

It might sound like I am beating the drum again, but the best thing in the world for employees, managers, and shareholders alike is a company that is doing well financially. That should be item one on the CEO's to do list if he wants to rebuild a sense of loyalty.

But I still believe that the seeds of a future loyalty movement rest within employee ownership. The more employees appreciate what holding stock in a company means, the more they think like owners, the more loyal they become.

That doesn't mean they are going to be easy to deal with.

The most loyal employees at United Airlines are the pilots, but their loyalty takes some unusual turns. They are very tough-minded in their contract negotiations, but their whole pitch, their whole mentality, is different than that of most employees. Almost anybody else at a company can shift jobs to a new employer and perhaps make more money. But pilots know that if they leave the company they will have to start at the bottom of the seniority ladder again, so they have an interest in staying at United. That means they want the company to be profitable and to continue to grow, because they know they will be at United for the long-term.

If you want to provide the atmosphere where loyalty at least has a chance, look to fair pay, to developing a company that employees can be proud of, to developing a company where the importance of job security is highly valued.

You need to make employees feel that they have finally arrived, and that after years of dedication and hard work, they can finally stop worrying about losing their jobs.

THIRTEEN

★

Paying Attention to the Right Things

The people who run corporations spend too much time paying too much attention to the wrong things.

In virtually every company I have worked for over four decades, I have seen executives spending just about all of their time on operations, on questions about producing a product or providing a service, on personnel, on cost cutting.

Those responsibilities seem to take up about 95 percent of everyone's time at the top of companies. What is left, that tiny 5 percent, is focused on a very important part of the business formula, the customer and marketing to the customer.

What happens because of this?

Car companies end up making cars people don't want. Retailers offer merchandise that doesn't sell in uncomfortable stores. Customers feel they are at the end of a long whip handled by characters who just don't seem to know or care how it feels to be lost and unhappy.

Airlines are a classic case.

Business flying is a lot of things, but pleasant doesn't rank very high on the list. I believe that is because everyone pays so much attention to the wrong things. It starts at the service counter and ends when the business traveler finally escapes the confusion of a big airport.

A very good cup of coffee might make the flight seem

a lot friendlier. A couple of more inches of legroom might help, too. Seats that actually recline on command instead of just slipping back when you don't expect it are important. ("Sir, your seat back must be upright for landing!" is the prompt. "It's broken," is the all too frequent response.)

A CEO might never have the chance to think about any of that as he pushes his way through the details that make up the daily life of a big company.

Placing so little emphasis on the customer is wrong.

But I know why it happens.

CEOs are trained by business schools or engineering schools or economics schools. They come to the workplace looking for ways to quantify just about everything because of those backgrounds. The operations side of a business, particularly a manufacturing business, is tangible and measurable.

Because of that, CEOs can become myopic and narrowly focused on getting the product out, comparing themselves with their competitors, and working on organizational and people plans. As part of that process, they lose sight of their customers, and that is unfortunate.

That is not all that is lost.

By focusing almost exclusively on what happens *inside* a company, a CEO also disconnects from what happens *outside*.

Losing the connection to the customer is the first symptom. And losing the connection to the community, to society, where corporations have the potential to make great contributions, is the second.

A CEO has responsibilities that go beyond what he might view as the business.

For me, that connection has stretched all the way from supporting the higher education of economically disadvantaged young people who might miss life's opportunities without some help, to working hard on the back-to-work side of welfare reform.

It's all too common for the people who head companies to complain about the problems and challenges of society. From the customer to the community, the emphasis should be the same: What are the problems? What are you going to do about them?

It amazes me that it is so easy to lose the connection to customers.

During my early days at Ford Motor Co., back in 1957, I watched another young man who had been assigned to Ford's tractor division. I didn't know him well but we had some conversations and I would see him at meetings. As a tractor product planner, his job was to help create the kinds of tractors farmers would want to buy.

There are a lot of ways to attack that kind of assignment. A planner can study the statistics, look at survey data, and pore over sales records to see what sold in the past. He can hire consultants and talk to marketing gurus. But this young character from my early days at Ford found what I still believe is a better model.

He spent days on end in his car on rural roads.

He would sit for hours watching farmers working the fields with their tractors. He would talk to them about the equipment, about what worked well and what didn't work well. What did they need to make their work easier and more efficient?

That is how he would create his tractor plans.

He said watching farmers work and talking to them about their machines was better for him than all the paper studies he had ever seen.

For me, it was an early and valuable lesson.

Go ask. Go watch. You will get your best ideas that way.

Lee Iacocca understood the focus on the customer.

He understood marketing, too.

He probably spent half his time with dealers trying to understand what they thought customers wanted. He spent a lot of time with advertising agencies, even helping with the copywriting on Chrysler ads.

If the boss limits himself only to inside challenges, he could well be missing out on a whole world of opportunity that waits just outside the building.

I have two stories that underline the importance of these outside connections.

One of them is about coffee and how important a good cup is to the frequent traveler (although the more important message is about the value of a strong brand name) and the second is about the day I came up with a plan to take over the world.

Well, it was not literally a plan to take over the world, but it could well become a plan to take United's customers anywhere they want to go in the world, which in the airline business is just about the same thing.

The same nugget of wisdom—paying attention to customers—rests at the heart of both of these stories.

Traditionally, airplanes were just big, efficient flying boxes to transport people. My thought was that we could make them a lot more pleasant, offer passengers more options than they have ever had before, and add new value to the old transportation formula.

First, java.

Starbucks Coffee has become just about ubiquitous.

Visit almost any big city, and not just in America, and it seems that cardboard cup with the distinctive insignia has become an essential part of the urban uniform.

Office workers of every stripe used to be known by their suits and their briefcases and their purposeful strides.

Now, they also need a great, portable grande latte to complete the picture.

To a student of business, the Starbucks story is one of the most amazing developments in decades.

Not so long ago, coffee was a generic cup of maybe okay

(and maybe not) beverage that you picked up at a diner or at a donut shop for a quarter—tops a half a buck.

Your options?

Cream and sugar.

If you wanted very good coffee, generally you got it at a very good restaurant, you made it at home, or you went to Europe, where café culture had developed the perfect cup.

Starbucks changed all of that.

And it changed it in such a compelling way that coffee suddenly became worth up to $3.50 a cup depending on the size of cup and the option you selected.

I got a call from Howard Schultz, the CEO at Starbucks, a few years ago. He wanted to talk about the value of a good brand. He had been in business for only about three years at the time, but Starbucks was already setting a standard in the coffee industry.

For some reason, he said, he was unable to get America's airlines to recognize they didn't have to serve that odious brown hot stuff that might or might not seem like coffee at thirty thousand feet.

I thought: "Good point. Why should airline coffee be so awful?"

I told him that I thought the value created by his brand was remarkable and I compared it to United's own brand value, which had taken us seventy years to nurture and develop and which also was powerful. It struck me at that point that, in the world of great brands, a company is known by the company it keeps.

In the back of my head was the thought that embracing someone else's brand could do a lot of good for a company like United, and a lot of good for that other brand, too.

What came of that conversation is apparent to anyone who flies United.

We serve Starbucks coffee on all of our flights.

There were some challenges.

Coffee brewed on terra firma isn't the same as coffee brewed at thirty thousand feet in a pressurized airplane cabin. But we figured out a way to solve that problem, made a partnership, and married two very strong brands, much to the benefit of our customers.

Taking over the world was a little more complicated.

In 1994, United had just completed forming an alliance with Lufthansa, the German airline. It was a good deal for both airlines. Even though United is the world's largest airline, there were still many cities around the world we didn't serve.

We had already decided to pay close attention to our business customers, and we knew that as international boundaries kept melting away and the world became a smaller and smaller place, it would be to our benefit to fly to a lot more cities.

We had 575 aircraft, and in terms of capacity that makes us the biggest airline in the world. But it is still not possible for United to fly everywhere.

But we realized in conversations with the German airline that we could craft an agreement where our most valued customers could make seamless transfers to Lufthansa. That would give them comfortable, dependable, and safe access to a lot more cities of the world.

Better yet, the agreement would allow United's customers to accumulate their frequent flyer miles when flying on Lufthansa.

Frequent flyer miles are just as good as money in the world of travel arrangements these days. Being able to accumulate United's miles on Lufthansa opened up a whole world of possibilities for air travelers.

It took a while for the alliance to function properly because of different computer systems and the challenge of getting one airline's culture and schedule to mesh properly with another's.

But it worked, because it was in the interest of the companies and their customers that it should work.

I went to Germany at Christmas of 1995 to celebrate this new partnership.

We were in talks with Air Canada at that point, looking to reach a similar agreement to give United's customers seamless access to their services, too. I decided it might be interesting to take the Air Canada people to Germany for the Christmas party.

At the same time, Lufthansa was involved in conversations with Scandinavian Air System (SAS) to work out a similar partnership with them. And we were both talking to Thai Airlines with the same goal in mind.

We partied and celebrated the season.

Then we sat down for coffee one afternoon as the visit was coming to an end. I looked at the CEOs of the other four airlines at the table and decided to be bold.

"We have the making of a multilateral alliance here," I said.

I wasn't quite clear about that in my own mind and I didn't know where the idea would take us.

But I had presented the idea and carried the thought with me.

In a matter of weeks, I was able to articulate what I thought we could accomplish by working together.

"None of us is big enough to serve all the principal cities of the world on our own," I said. "United would have to triple in size to do that. And more and more cities are going to become destinations because business is becoming more and more global."

I suggested a simple but multilateral alliance, along the lines of the United-Lufthansa agreement.

I was thinking of how I would explain this to customers.

"If you normally fly on United and we don't go where you want to go, we will get you there in our alliance system with one seamless connection. If you are one of our frequent flyers, we will treat you better with upgrades and access to our lounges. And our partner airlines will give you that special treatment, too. We will keep a high standard for safety. Each airline in the alliance will have its own standards of service, based on its culture, but if you are a United customer, you can rest assured you will be safe and warmly welcomed."

You might think that an arrangement like this one would be exceedingly complicated. Think about the lawyers. Think about the structure you would have to create to make it work well.

Not at all.

We agreed at the beginning that we would keep this as simple as possible. There were no big teams of international lawyers involved. Partners in the alliance signed a five-page agreement.

The alliance airlines are not handcuffed to one another. If they find over time that they are not getting the financial benefit they want, first they talk to the other partners to see how that problem can be addressed. But ultimately, they are free to withdraw from the alliance if it doesn't work for them and their customers.

The right to leave is the magnet that holds us all together. We all try harder to share the extra profit and the extra flying.

It took us about a year to get the system working.

We conducted surveys all over the world and came up with what we believed was a great name: Star Alliance. It now includes thirteen airline partners almost filling out the globe and it has done exactly what was intended. It serves our customers well and it brings us all more business and more places to fly.

Using new software, United and its partners are working on refinements.

For example, we want to establish a Web page that will allow customers anywhere in the world to check on their frequent flyer status across all our companies. That means we have to figure out how to get thirteen computer systems to talk to one another. We now have thirty people assigned to the various software tasks.

But Star Alliance doesn't have a fat, traditional management structure. It is operated by a series of committees among the airlines.

So where did that alliance idea really come from?

The telephone.

Make a call to Singapore and think about what happens.

There could be six independent telephone companies involved in completing that call, but the customer couldn't care less. He doesn't have to make arrangements to shift from company A to company B and beyond.

He wants a clear channel to the person he is calling and one bill that summarizes the costs.

Star Alliance does the same thing.

It takes much of the hassle out of making arrangements and flying just about anywhere in the world.

It is not yet perfect.

Lufthansa and United don't share the same terminal at Heathrow Airport in London, for example. That means a traveler gets off a plane, takes a bus to another terminal, and then gets on another plane. We are currently negotiating in dozens of airports, Heathrow among them, to simplify that process by locating Star Alliance airlines in the same terminals.

Star Alliance is going to be crucial as United works to rebuild its relationships with customers in the wake of last summer's cancellations and delays. Making the process of world travel easier and more efficient will help rebuild those ties that keep people coming back, trip after trip.

It will take some time, but it will happen.

Think of how complicated it would have been if we started with all the lawyers and all the airport authorities first and put Star Alliance on hold until we had negotiated terminal space.

It would have taken years.

When you have a good idea, go with it.

I have watched simple ideas transform business for decades.

You never quite know where a good idea will carry you.

Car rebates are a case in point.

At some point, some executives at Chrysler decided they would give rebates on cars to move some inventory. Now just about everyone gives rebates. It has changed the car industry because it allows manufacturers to change prices fast and frequently.

It has even changed banking.

Not so long ago, if you wanted a car loan, you had to be able to present, say, 20 percent of the car price as a down payment to get the loan. Now often you just go to the bank and hand over that rebate check.

It's not even your own money.

But boy, does it move cars.

Frequent flyer miles had the same impact.

American Airlines invented them as a short-term promotion, but they were so successful that they became an industry staple. For a big airline, they have become a crucial part of the business, something that wasn't anticipated but that represents a major change.

In both cases, no one knew where those ideas would lead when they were hatched. But almost everyone saw their value right away and found a way to run with them.

It is no coincidence that both of those ideas were sharply focused on the needs and interests of customers. Address your challenges at that level, and your business will succeed.

The minivan experience, which actually began at a very reluctant Ford Motor Co. and then came to life later at Chrysler, is another case in point.

There just wasn't much survey data to support the introduction of minivans. Potential customers would look at mock-ups and shudder. What is this supposed to be, a truck, an expanded car, an inflated station wagon? A monster bread basket? Despite those reactions, the car planners who were most infatuated with the idea of minivans pressed on.

And the marketplace eventually told them they were absolutely right.

Sometimes, you just have to go with your gut, but that is tough.

The toughest marketing problems that I have ever encountered came when I was dealing with a product that was so new that the public just didn't know yet that it wanted it.

It takes extraordinary confidence to move ahead in those situations.

I think today's obvious example is the Internet.

How could the public give the Internet industry the answers that it wanted when the public didn't even know what the Internet was? But that industry is developing at the speed of light. We still don't know where it is going to carry us, but it is clear that this is one of those businesses with vast potential.

It's one of those places where the gut feeling outweighs the available research.

It didn't take a marketing guru to know that a great cup of coffee would add value for travelers on United Airlines. And it didn't take an army of consultants and attorneys to recognize that our customers would love it if we could find an easier way to connect them to the world that had become their workplace.

Good ideas can come from just about anyplace. I was always bombarded with suggestions and complaints in the car business and the airline business. I was often asked if I objected to being recognized on a flight. Unless I was exhausted, I always liked talking to passengers and getting ideas. On my way from New York to Chicago once, I sat next to a recent Kellogg grad, Allison Katz, who found out who I was and said, "Hey, how about bottled water in economy class; you can take something off to save room and weight." I thought it was a great idea. Sara Fields, our senior vice president for on-board services, liked the idea and we did it.

I have had some great marketing ideas over the past forty years, but I have had my regrets, too.

Here is one that is going to sound a little strange.

I regret that I wasn't flashier.

Yes, flashier.

It is difficult for me to admit this because it runs counter to the way I think about almost everything.

In speaking to customers, flash really does work.

Lee Iacocca had flash. I didn't. I had diligence. I had determination. I even had smarts. And okay, I flash sometimes.

But I never had real flash.

I have been denying the importance of flash for forty years.

But in a world in which so many messages are being sent to consumers so many different ways, in a world of "hurry up" sound bites, I must now admit that flash is the magical substance that can cut through all the mush and send the clearest message.

Richard Branson, the fellow who runs Virgin Atlantic.

Now, there is flash.

This man is all marketing. He is all arms and legs and the more outrageous he is, the more people believe that Virgin Atlantic and everything connected to it is just wonderful.

Put it to the test.

I have.

I said to people, "United is a very big airline. We have 575 aircraft. How big is Virgin Atlantic?"

They say, "Well, a hundred airplanes? Maybe seventy-five airplanes?"

When I told them it's eighteen airplanes and growing to twenty-three, the reaction was almost always the same, "Come on, you have got to be kidding."

But that company is run by someone who is bigger than life, and it pays off.

There are some people in this world who can live their

life on four hours of sleep and work seven days, and those
are the kinds of guys who can have flash and also do the
business part.

That makes a difference.

Looking back, I think Ed Molina, that wonderful character who was my boss at Ford and who delighted in life
and work, had flash.

Some companies do so well they don't need flash at the
top.

General Electric doesn't need flash.

Microsoft doesn't need flash at all, but it has it.

I have been to conferences with Bill Gates.

What unusual flash that man has. He plays the role of
brilliant nerd, and he plays it so well.

Warren Buffett doesn't have any flash.

But he plays this anti-flash role very well.

"If I were looking at Berkshire," he will write in his annual reports, "I would never invest here. I screwed up. I
made a big mistake."

Of course, he has also achieved an enormous return for
his shareholders, a performance louder than flash itself.

I spent so many years thinking of flash as something su-
perficial that it is difficult for me to recognize how important it is today. As a marketing tool, it works.

I'm not going to argue whether that is fair or just,
whether substance should count for more.

The importance of flash is that it reaches past everything
else and speaks directly to customers who do not want to
take the time to understand substance, and that is a tool
you just can't buy. You have to have it.

Sometimes, I must admit, it's just not a fair world.

FOURTEEN

--------------------★--------------------

How Not to Sell Your Soul

I love big ideas.

The bigger, the better.

As my time at United Airlines was coming to a close, I looked over two documents that had been sitting on my desk for a few days. They were both about a genuinely big idea.

But they were also about corporate responsibility, and the individual responsibilities of the people who run big companies.

Responsibility does not stop in the workplace.

The responsibility of the individual and of the corporation stretches out into society. It is easy to forget society's problems when you have a fat salary, great stock options, and a pile of money in the bank.

Money can insulate you from just about everything.

It can buy distance from other people's problems and provide that beautiful house on the hill, with its own reality inside.

But success has another, more important role.

It can carry a company, and an individual, right into the heart of problems. An individual with experience, a company that is successful, can use intelligence, resources, and goodwill to attack trouble outside the corporation.

For most of my career, I have watched as the United

States, through good intentions gone wrong, constructed one of history's biggest welfare systems.

How many generations have been born into dependency during the forty years I worked as an executive? How many brilliant young men and women have been lost in that artificial world, with its disconnection from comfortable, promising America?

As I said, I like big ideas.

One of my biggest ideas has been to help find a way to break that cycle of welfare dependency and help this new generation find its way into a different, better, and productive life. I know the value of climbing those mountains. I know what that did for me.

I had a lot of help along the way, and a few years ago, I decided it was time for me, and time for United Airlines, to reach out and help some other people start the climb, too.

That's what these two documents are all about.

The first is an address to Stanford's Graduate School of Business in January 1999, when I knew I would be leaving United and wanted to send a message to all those future executives who would be following me into CEO jobs well into the twenty-first century.

The second is a Harvard Business School study that I am proud of. It tells the story of United's role in the welfare to work effort.

It presents a powerful lesson about the effect corporations can have when they realize that their obligations don't stop with employees and customers and shareholders.

I have always been bothered by the assumption that there was some kind of disconnect between making good profits and doing good works.

Just as the historic bitterness between management and labor still poisons the atmosphere in corporate suites all over America today, that cliché of the heartless businessman obsessed only with personal profit also persists.

I know United isn't like that.

Our universe reaches beyond headquarters, beyond airlines, and certainly beyond that cliché about the heartlessness of business.

The United Foundation adopted a fifth-grade class of economically disadvantaged children in the city of Chicago. We offered a promise to their parents or guardians. If the kids stay in school and graduate, we will pay the costs of tuition for a four-year education at any Illinois state university.

Think of what that means in terms of opportunity, in terms of the contributions those children will make to their communities, to their families, to their society, as time passes.

If it sounds like a small-scale effort, I suppose it is when you think about how many children in how many big-city schools won't have that opportunity.

But it is certainly not small-scale in the lives of the families it will help.

United's commitment didn't stop there.

We donate air travel to parents of critically ill children who need to travel for medical treatment. We are a founding sponsor of ORBIS, which provides sight-saving surgery and medical training around the world.

Muscular dystrophy, Alzheimer's, breast cancer, Make-A-Wish, UNICEF, we participate in all of those associations. United employees even started their own program to provide in-home care for senior citizens and the disabled, called the NEED Foundation.

We have enlisted our customers in our giving programs with Charity Miles and Change the World with Your Change. Some frequent travelers accumulate more free miles than they can use and United provides a means to donate free miles to charities, either to provide travel for those who are ill but can't afford to fly to hospitals for treatment, or for sale by the charities.

At my last count, the program had given over 30 million miles.

International travelers are encouraged to donate foreign coins and small bills that are converted to dollars and donated as well.

These are all examples of what a strong company can do when it views its mission broadly.

As it turned out, we had a much bigger project in our future, too, a project that could well change the way America thinks and works in the twenty-first century.

It is, indeed, a giant-killer of a project.

I was called to the White House toward the end of 1996 by President Clinton to help craft a strategy for the nation's shift away from welfare dependency. Congress and state legislatures all over the country had made it clear that "welfare as we know it" would die.

The immediate challenge would be to come up with jobs that would move welfare recipients into the workforce.

The result was the Welfare to Work Partnership.

The president mentioned it in his State of the Union address in 1997, naming United Airlines, Sprint, Burger King, Monsanto, and United Parcel Service as leaders of the effort.

I was named chairman.

Eli Segal, who ran Americorps, became the full-time director of the Welfare to Work Partnership. This was a blessing. He was so creative, so hardworking, that he took a lot of the burden from me so that I could have the time to fulfill my responsibilities at United and at the partnership.

We were to build a partnership of large and small businesses committed to hiring, training, and supporting welfare recipients, without displacing the people who were already on our payrolls.

I recognize that this probably sounds like one of those do-gooder efforts that involve a lot of public relations and not much action. But that isn't how the Welfare to Work Partnership turned out.

It is not charity, it is not do-gooderism, and it is not philanthropy.

It's really all about business.

Welfare to work became a bottom-line decision that can make companies stronger. And it allowed United Airlines to play a leading role, establishing a model other businesses could turn to so they could develop their own welfare to work efforts.

In the process, welfare to work is helping to solve a difficult problem that has been hounding society for decades. It breaks people out of those cycles of dependency that had frozen them in place for so long.

I had my doubts at the beginning, even though I was praising the effort to the skies, performing missionary work all over the country, and finding converts wherever I could.

After all, I didn't create the welfare problem.

My partners in the program and I could well have concluded it was government's job to clean up its own mess.

Then there were all those ugly assumptions about welfare recipients, that all they wanted was a government check, that they didn't want to work, that they just couldn't be responsible.

People still have those old welfare stories in their heads.

I didn't believe them then and I don't believe them now.

But anyone who has dealt with culture in as many different places as I have knows how hard it is to cast some truth and reality against those old clichés.

I feared I would face a big challenge selling this effort to corporate America.

"Greenwald," that little voice in my head kept saying, "what have you gotten yourself into?"

Was it a smart business decision that would help United get good employees who would recognize the importance of sticking with us? Would the business community really buy it? Would welfare recipients choose a paycheck over a welfare check? Would the program have staying power?

It took a lot of work.

My pitch to corporate America was a simple one.

The United States simply cannot be a great nation if it embraces an "I'm okay, tough luck for you" philosophy. I argued that welfare reform was only going to work if the people who have done so well, the companies that have done so well, step up to the plate and make a commitment.

Times are good, I said, which means it's the right moment to attack this problem. We had the jobs, the expertise, and the time to focus. We could either keep complaining about welfare and its problems, or we could do something about it.

The government was certainly serious. It had created a number of incentives to encourage businesses to hire welfare recipients. It also set aside $750 million in Department of Labor grants to support innovative welfare to work programs in 1998 and 1999.

Those voices of doubt are becoming quieter now.

I know that welfare to work does work, all over the nation. I know it is a smart solution for businesses of all sizes, because I know they are stronger because they have hired and kept welfare recipients on the job.

And most important of all, I know that, when given the chance, former welfare recipients become dedicated and reliable employees.

We started out with those five vanguard companies. Now the project has more than twenty thousand participating companies. Over 1,100,000 former welfare recipients have been hired, and it's only a start.

I am well aware that the program has hit its share of bumps. Some efforts have collapsed. Helping people to change lives that have been going in the wrong direction, in some cases for generations, isn't easy. The welfare to work campaign has created its share of missteps, particularly in cases in which there hasn't been enough follow-up, or enough of the level of diligence we have tried to apply at United Airlines.

But some of the news has been very good.

Being obsessive about the value of research, I was in-

trigued by the results of a Wirthlin Group survey on the
project.

It found:

- Eight of ten business owners who have hired former
  welfare recipients say their new hires are "good, productive employees."
- A diverse collection of companies reports higher retention rates for welfare to work employees than for
  more traditional entry-level workers.

At United, we found that our retention rates for welfare
to work employees were almost twice as high as retention
rates for our other workers.

We started off with modest plans at United. We set a goal
of hiring four hundred former welfare recipients in 1997,
and we were afraid that even that might be a stretch. But
we found that the quality of candidates was so high that we
blew that goal away. We are well on the way to reaching our
long-term goal of two thousand former welfare recipients
on the payroll.

That didn't happen without some help, though.

And this is where corporate experience played a very important role, along with some very good intentions on the
part of United.

I didn't order anyone to do it. Our employees came forward. They liked the idea of helping welfare recipients
move into jobs, but they knew that kind of effort would require structure. They asked only to be freed up to create
what was needed.

They set up their own welfare to work task team early in
1997. It took them just two months to launch United's program.

We talked a lot about what kind of landing zone we
needed to provide for welfare recipients. All welfare recipients are not the same. Some have high school diplomas or
beyond and are ready for work. Some need help getting

GEDs and catching up on the basics. And some, particularly those who had never had the experience of working, needed a little more help.

Most of all, we didn't want to create a separate class of employees. We wanted to move the welfare to work people into the normal workplace as quickly and as efficiently as possible. They would face the same work challenges, the same conditions, as their fellow workers.

It took a lot of technical training to achieve that goal. No one just walks onto a job on the United ramp at the airport, or into a flight attendant's position, or to a reservations desk. We provided the same rigorous training for these folks as we did for all of our new hires. They had to pass the same tests and meet the same standards.

We anticipated some bumps, and we certainly hit them.

Salary was a problem. Because of our status as an employee-owned company, our pay rates for beginning workers were not very high. Our employees were getting company stock, but had taken pay cuts in return.

We were concerned that shortly after we completed our extensive training programs, our new employees would be lured to other airlines paying higher salaries. These were folks who needed a paycheck. Stock to be held for retirement was not a compelling attraction.

But we did have a good argument.

We told them we had no intention of providing short-term jobs. United Airlines would be a career for them, offering many long-term career opportunities.

And we had something else, too.

Mentoring has been one of the strongest and most effective components of welfare to work at United.

Everyone needs a friend when a new job begins.

I had mine at Ford, Chrysler, United, and everywhere else I have ever worked.

We decided to make that process more formal at United because we knew it would help us retain our new employees.

We asked for employee volunteers to serve as company mentors to each of our new welfare to work employees.

Sometimes they are cheerleaders and sometimes they are sounding boards. Sometimes they just provide good workplace advice. But the mentoring program is why we have such a high retention rate for welfare to work employees.

How did that make us stronger?

Our people who worked with those new employees got their own education. I believe they found a new appreciation for their own jobs.

That improvement in attitude plays out where it is most important for United Airlines, at the customer service level.

I think that in welfare to work projects all over the country, we have demolished that old cliché about welfare recipients, that they don't want to work or that they aren't up to the challenges of the job.

The other cliché that crumbled in the process was the assumption that good works and good business are mutually exclusive.

They are not.

The choice is not between working for profit or working for purpose.

The choice is to work for profit *and* for purpose.

I didn't know that in 1957 when I walked out of Princeton and into Ford Motor Co.

You truly do live and learn, but how much you live and how much you learn is a function of where life carries you.

I started out as an eager and ambitious young man, always ready to advance, always ready to face the next challenge, climb the next mountain.

I was very lucky because, even though there were some uncomfortable moments of downtime between jobs, when I realized that what I needed in my life was work, that next opportunity always came along.

In the process, I learned that I certainly did not know it

all. My career as an executive would actually become a reflection of the careers and jobs of the people I worked with over many years.

I did well because they were kind enough to teach me well.

Forty years is a long time, but somehow these days, it doesn't seem quite long enough.

I said goodbye to my friends at United during the annual shareholder meeting in Denver in May of 1999. I am certainly not sad about it, and I had the great advantage of leaving a company that is strong and has the prospects of getting a lot stronger.

The place was just about on the ropes when I arrived, and we brought it back together.

You bet it was an emotional moment.

I look at where United Airlines is going and I sometimes wish I had twenty more years so I could grow with it, just to see where all that potential will lead.

I think back on the dark days at Chrysler, and on that moment when we knew we had saved the place. If we had not succeeded, 500,000 lives would have been tossed into turmoil.

I have the same feeling about Ford and rambling all over the world.

As Humphrey Bogart says in *Casablanca*, We'll always have Paris.

This journey of mine has been a great privilege. It's not over yet, I realized as I was finishing this book. The greatest lesson of my life has been that love from and for family is the best of all enrichments.

Glenda continues to learn and grow with me. She is now determined to bring together Asian, Alternative, and Western medicine to encourage practitioners to choose the best from all three.

Our oldest son, Scott, is a top manager at a Ford dealership in a Latino area of Los Angeles. He and his wife, Julie, have two wonderful children. Our daughter, Stacey, is a real New Yorker and professional architect. Brad, our third child, is married to Rachel and lives in Denver, where he is a senior executive of an Internet start-up. They also have two wonderful children. Josh, our fourth child, is a broker who sells hotels and lives in Boston.

They didn't have roots in one place or one neighborhood, and so their best friends are each other.

New mountains continue to thrill me. But more of the time these days they are actual mountains in Colorado. I am trying to stay fit. I run a lot. I am returning to tennis. Business still thrills me and I have formed a merchant bank with two former Goldman Sachs folks, Joel Beckman and Regg Jones.

I still feel the need, actually the obligation, to help others. I live in the most privileged period in the history of the world, one of the most privileged people in a privileged country.

I was thinking about all that when I talked to the Stanford Business School graduates several months ago.

It might have seemed a strange place to be talking about philanthropy. These young people were at Stanford to learn all about how to make lots of money, not about how to give it away.

But I wanted them to understand the most important lesson of all, something they could carry with them into the twenty-first century, a lesson that might help them decide how they should live.

I told them they could walk out of the place with their MBAs under their arms and live out that old cliché about business graduates: "Make money and the hell with everything else."

But after forty years and after making a lot of money, I wanted to present some other options.

I told them it is fine to use your brain and your talents to make a lot of money, but you can have purpose in your lives, too. Chase the excitement of a new economy, make big bucks, but don't forget to help those who have been left behind.

When you stop at age sixty-five, as I have to get my thoughts into this book, you will realize that you can have your excitement and money from business, and you can make a contribution to your society.

That way, both your mind and your soul will be satisfied.

INDEX